How To
ACHIEVE
YOUR
POTENTIAL
And
Enjoy Life!

STEVE DOUGLASS
AND AL JANSSEN

 Here's Life Publishers

Published by
HERE'S LIFE PUBLISHERS
P.O. Box 1576
San Bernardino, CA 92402-1576

HLP Product No. 951822

Library of Congress Cataloging-in-Publication Data
Douglass, Stephen B.
How to Achieve your potential and Enjoy Life
     1. Self-realization   2. Conduct of life.
3. Witness Bearing (Christianity) I. Janssen, Al.
II. Title
BJ1470.D68   1987   248.8'4   86-33665
ISBN 0-89840-184-4 (pbk.)

FOR MORE INFORMATION, WRITE:

L.I.F.E. — P.O. Box A399, Sydney South 2000, Australia
Campus Crusade for Christ of Canada — Box 300, Vancouver, B.C., V6C 2X3, Canada
Campus Crusade for Christ — Pearl Assurance House, 4 Temple Row, Birmingham, B2 5HG, England
Campus Crusade for Christ — P.O. Box 240, Colombo Court Post Office, Singapore 9117
Lay Institute for Evangelism — P.O. Box 8786, Auckland 3, New Zealand
Great Commission Movement of Nigeria — P.O. Box 500, Jos, Plateau State Nigeria, West Africa
Campus Crusade for Christ International — Arrowhead Springs, San Bernardino, CA 92414, U.S.A.

You *Can* Achieve Your Potential

Let Steve Douglass, a Harvard MBA, executive vice president of a multi-national corporation, and seminar speaker, guide you to the principles that will help you:

- Determine what you *really* want to accomplish in life
- Gain control of your schedule and organize your home and workplace
- Develop meaningful, enjoyable relationships
- Achieve new levels of skill and knowledge
- Conquer worry through three powerful techniques
- Live with a genuine sense of security, hope and peace

. . . and Enjoy Life!

Other Here's Life books by Steve Douglass

How to Get Better Grades and Have More Fun
Managing Yourself
The Ministry of Management

Other Here's Life books by Al Janssen

Fast Break: Heroes of the NBA
Breakaway: Heroes of the NHL

CONTENTS

1. A UNIQUE PROJECT 9

One neighborhood decides to find out how much they can do to help one another achieve their potential and enjoy life.

2. THE FINISH LINE 18

How to establish and achieve objectives for your life and career.

3. TIME TO GET ORGANIZED 29

Some practical ways to gain control of your schedule and organize your home and office.

4. RELATING TO PEOPLE 41

Caring for people, listening to them and affirming them. Three keys to more effective, enjoyable relationships.

5. EXPANDED HORIZONS 50

One of the secrets to personal growth . . . exploring new areas of knowledge and skill, and selecting those that are right for you.

6. ROLL WITH THE BENEFITS 62

How to achieve your potential and enjoy life even when you are interrupted "all the time."

7. INCREASING THE FOLLOW THROUGH 71

Beyond good intentions to persistence, accountability and discipline.

8. SPEAKING YOUR MIND 81

How you can tell others what you feel and think in a clear, positive way.

9. THE SEARCH FOR PEACE 91

When the bottom falls out, where can you find hope and peace that sustain you?

10. STRATEGIES TO HANDLE WORRY 98

Three powerful ways to deal with the anxiety that robs your energy.

11. ICE CREAM ACTIVITIES 106

Learning to like what you have to do.

12. PUTTING IT ALL TOGETHER 114

The neighborhood finds out how far they have progressed in helping one another achieve their potential and enjoy life.

Appendix A 127
Appendix B 132
Appendix C 134

*to Michelle
and
to Jonathan*

Any book is the product of the efforts of many people, not just the authors. The following are people who played a special role in this book. To them we would like to say a special word of thanks:

To Judy Douglass and Jo Janssen, our wives, for their help and encouragement.

To Barb Hoffman and Debbie Austin for their long hours of typing.

To Dan Benson and Barb Sherrill of Here's Life Publishers for their artful and accurate editing.

To Ray Moore and Russell Barr for their excellent illustration and layout.

To Larry Thompson for his attractive cover design.

To Terry Smith of Here's Life Publishers for her faithful coordination of production.

One neighborhood decides to
find out how much they can do
to help one another achieve their
potential and enjoy life.

1

A UNIQUE PROJECT

C lark wanted to be a better salesman.

Sue was frustrated by constant interruptions from her preschool children.

Sam was tired of his job and wanted to make a career change.

Julie desired a deeper relationship with her husband.

And Alice . . . well, she was a recently divorced mother of three who'd just moved into the neighborhood. Everything was going wrong in her new house. Alice's problems helped Clark, Sue, Sam, and Julie solve their problems.

Sound unusual? Well, it happened on Fir Court. That's one of a series of streets that radiate off Jackson Avenue in a suburb of a large city. What happened to these people was dramatically life-changing. But it could have happened in any neighborhood, because most people have the same basic desires.

"What desires?" you ask. The desire to be successful. To feel significant. To find fulfillment. To experience satisfaction with life. To love and be loved. To have hope for a better life. To have peace of mind and contentment. In a few words — to achieve their potential and enjoy life.

Most of us don't talk openly about these desires. But they simmer just below the surface and influence our decisions, activities and relationships.

So if anyone came along who could help us achieve our potential and enjoy life, we'd probably listen to him, wouldn't we? That's exactly what happened among the neighbors on Fir Court.

These people might have existed like most neighborhoods, talking about the weather and occasionally borrowing each other's tools or an egg or a cup of sugar. That this neighborhood was different was due primarily to the perceptive insight of a man who had a goal. His ambition was to help people achieve their maximum potential in life — particularly his neighbors on Fir Court.

His name was Ted Simpson, a prematurely gray-haired man in his early forties. He was national sales training manager for a respected insurance company. His wife was a piano teacher. Together, they had a strong desire to succeed in every area of their lives. They wanted to achieve their potential, and they wanted to help those around them — particularly their three children — achieve their potential. One result was that people enjoyed being around them, and life for Ted and Amy was an exciting adventure.

One of the first things they did after all the homes were occupied in the new housing development was organize a get-acquainted neighborhood potluck and barbecue. It happened on a muggy Sunday evening in July. There were hamburgers and hot dogs with all the trimmings, potato salad, cold slaw, jello salads, watermelon, and an assortment of baked delights. All this took place on the Simpsons' driveway and front lawn, the middle of the seven homes on the cul-de-sac.

Ted and Amy made sure Alice Davies felt welcomed. She had just moved with her three kids into the last vacant house on the block less than twenty-four hours earlier. "Thanks for inviting me," said Alice with a smile. "My kids would have had peanut butter and jelly sandwiches tonight."

Normally Alice was a fairly organized person, but this move had taxed her limits. She had hesitated when Amy issued the invitation because she was unable to contribute any food to the potluck on such short notice. "There will be plenty of food," Amy had insisted. "Just come and don't worry about bringing anything."

Alice was more than a little frustrated by the condition of her new house. She'd discovered that the washing machine didn't work, there was a leak under one bathroom sink, the air conditioning was either too warm or too cold, and one of the bedroom doors stuck so badly that it required a "shoulder block" to open. If that wasn't enough, her car had chosen this weekend to start misfiring. "Are all the houses on this block as well-made as mine?" she asked with a sigh.

"I'm afraid so," Ted chuckled. "As soon as you buy 'em, it's time to fix 'em. Seriously, though, once the bugs are worked out, these are good homes." Ted had noted the frustration in Alice's voice and wondered if there was a way to find her some help — fast. It had to be frustrating to move in alone, try to fix up the house, supervise three kids, and maintain a job.

Ted and Amy made it a point to get acquainted with everyone. They had already gotten to know Clark and Sue Appleton who lived on the southeast corner of the block, next door to Alice. Clark sold athletic equipment to schools. "Did you see the ball game this afternoon?" Clark asked while he helped Ted flip hamburgers. "The Braves came from behind in the last inning to win!"

Ted enjoyed sports, though he wasn't a fanatic. "Are you a Braves fan?" Ted asked.

"I enjoy them because they're on the tube almost every day. I've got one of those big screen TVs; it's almost like being at the ball park. You'll have to come over and watch sometime."

The Turners lived directly across the street from the Appletons. Sam was as intense as Clark was relaxed. His wife, Julie, introduced Ken, a son by Sam's first marriage, to the Simpsons. "You going to school?" asked Ted.

"I attended junior college last year," Ken answered. "But right now I'm working a highway construction job."

"And eating us out of house and home," quipped Sam. "Some day he'll discover what he wants to do with his life."

"Yeah, just like my dad. He hates his job but he's stuck. I'm not going to fall into that trap." Ted took note of the exchange and wondered how he might be able to help them expand their vision and realize the potential they had in life.

Next door to the Turners lived two single women, Angela and Robin. Ted and Amy learned that Angela was an engineer who worked for the state highway division. "Is this your first home?" Amy asked.

"Yes. Up to now, I've always lived in apartments. I thought it'd be a good investment to buy a house and have a roommate who would pay rent to help with my payments." She introduced her roommate, Robin, a shy young lady who revealed only that she had a job as a secretary.

Between the single women and the Simpsons lived Bob and Ginny Harris. Amy and Ginny had chatted briefly as neighbors but Ted had not had an opportunity to interact with Bob. "What do you do for a living?" Ted asked.

"I'm an assistant district attorney for the county," he answered.

Bob seemed uncomfortable in the group and he wouldn't meet Ted's gaze.

"Sounds like a challenging job."

"It has its moments, but a lot is pretty routine. I've got five more years before I can take early retirement." He noted that a group of kids had finished eating and were playing ball in the streets. "Sure are a lot of kids around here."

"You have any children of your own?"

"We have a son. He's married and lives in Southern California."

"Grandchildren?"

"Two boys." Ted realized that Bob wasn't comfortable talking about himself, and didn't pressure his neighbor. As people began to dig into the desserts, Bob and Ginny excused themselves. "My husband's not feeling well," Ginny whispered to Amy. "He needs to get to sleep early so he's ready for work in the morning."

After carving a watermelon, Ted took a large wedge and sat down next to his neighbor who lived immediately to the east, Manny Riess. Manny was a truck driver and his wife, Carol, a legal secretary. They were the youngest couple on the block, not yet in their thirties. Manny carried a 35 millimeter camera around his neck and had already shot a roll of film, primarily candid shots of the neighborhood children.

Ted noted that Manny had a generous supply of cookies, brownies, and cakes on his paper plate. "Everything looked so good," Manny said with a grin. "Had to try one of everything." Carol, meanwhile, was content with a small slice of watermelon and one cookie.

Alice was the next person to excuse herself. "I hate to eat and run, but I've still got a lot to do tonight, and I'd like to get a little sleep before I have to go back to work in the morning."

What happened next was the spark that started a chain reaction that forever changed this from an ordinary neighborhood. Sue Appleton asked, "Is there anything I can do to help?"

Alice didn't want to admit she could use some help, and said good-naturedly, "Don't worry, I'll survive."

But Sue was persistent. "I'd really like to help. I could unpack some boxes for you, or help put things away."

A blush rose in Alice's face, but she was grateful for the offer. "Well, if it isn't an inconvenience, I really could use some help."

Ted saw his opportunity. "Alice, I hope you don't mind my mentioning that you have a couple of things that aren't working in your home . . ."

"Only a couple!" said Clark. "You're lucky."

"I'd like to see if I can fix your washing machine and that leak in your bathroom. Also, you said that one of your doors sticks real badly, and your car's been acting up . . ."

"I'd be glad to take a look at the car," said Manny.

Ken volunteered to fix the door. "Sounds like it may have swelled a bit in this heat," he said.

"I don't believe this," Alice sighed as she sat back down at the picnic table. "You all are so kind."

"Hey, what are neighbors for, anyway?" Clark said. "Right now, you need some help. Someday, maybe Sue and I will need a hand. If we don't help each other out, who will?"

"Is there anything I can do to help?" asked Angela.

"Thanks, but I'm sure that's enough for now."

"Say, I have an idea!" said Ted. He had decided this might be a golden opportunity to move toward a long-term dream. "I'm really excited about what I see happening here. Not every block has neighbors who help each other like this. And that gives me an idea that I'd like to propose to you.

"Obviously, all of us have experienced some success or we wouldn't be living here. Yet I would imagine all of us are looking for better ways to do our various activities. So we're constantly learning. In fact, one of my goals is to achieve my full potential as a person and help others who want to do the same. So that's why I'd like to propose a project that shouldn't take much of our time, but I think we'd all find helpful and a lot of fun."

Ted paused for a moment to see if he had everyone's attention. He knew his idea was unusual, yet he felt confident that it was worthwhile. "I sense that each of you have things you can teach me that will help me learn how to come closer to my potential as a father, as a husband, as a neighbor, and in my work. Over the next year, I'd like to get to know each of you better — to brainstorm with you, to make observations — and keep track of what I learn in a notebook. Then about this time next year I'd share with you what I've learned."

"What kind of things are you looking for?" Julie asked.

"Anything that can help us live a more fulfilling and productive life. For example, how can we maximize our time? How can we strengthen relationships at work and home? How can we set realistic goals and discipline ourselves to reach those goals? How can we deal constructively with worry? How can we accomplish those unpleasant tasks in life?"

"Like getting around to all the things we should do?" Clark quipped.

"That's right. Maybe you find it hard to stay on top of that, but someone else may have a great method that would help you. The idea is that individually each of us has, no doubt, learned some things in all of these areas. If we pooled our information, all of us would benefit. We'd be more effective, come closer to realizing our potential, and probably enjoy life more."

"Sounds like a great idea!" Angela said.

"Are you going to interview us?" asked Sam, who wasn't sure he was comfortable with this unusual project.

"Well, I do like to ask questions," Ted acknowledged with a smile. "But I promise I won't put you on the spot. No one should feel obligated. By the way, I did a similar project a few years ago with some fellow insurance agents. As we interacted, we discovered we had similar struggles. As we shared ideas, we found we helped each other become better salespeople. All of us increased our production. My idea is that we could do that more generally. For example, several of us have kids. I know I could use some ideas on being a better parent, especially with my teenagers."

"I hear you," said Alice, who had a daughter in junior high. "I swear that my oldest girl has become a different person in the last year. It's not easy being a good parent, trying to keep a home, and also doing a quality job at work. I, for one, wouldn't mind learning how to balance all that. Is it really possible to reach my potential in all of those areas?"

"That's what I'd like to find out," Ted reported. "I believe we can. But we tend to get so wrapped up in the pressures of life, and trying to balance all of our roles, that it's hard to find time just to stop and think, *How can I do it better?*"

"What about Bob and Ginny Harris?" asked Angela.

"I hope they'll participate, too . . . if they want to."

"I don't know what I can contribute," said Sam, "but I'm willing to go along with the idea. It sounds intriguing . . . and it might help us draw closer together as neighbors."

So it was settled. While no one knew what to expect, there was a sense of anticipation that this was going to be a special neighborhood. Manny, Ken, and Sue went with Alice to her home. Clark intercepted Ted and said, "I'd sure like to know what you learned in your project with that group of agents . . . if it's not a secret."

"Not at all. Why don't you and Sue come over some evening this week?"

"Maybe you could have dinner with us," Amy suggested.

Ted didn't really want to assume the role of "teacher," but in Clark he saw someone who was where he had been ten years earlier. So perhaps this would get the process started.

* * *

Later that night, after cleaning up from the party, Ted and Amy reflected on the evening. Ted reported how Manny had discovered a cracked distributor cap in Alice's car and arranged to pick up a new one the next day at an auto supply shop. Ken had shaved the top of the sticky door. "Sue was helping Alice unpack and store her dishes when I left."

"Were you able to fix the washing machine?"

"Wasn't much to fix. Just a bad connection on the start button. The leaky pipe didn't take long to fix either. But she'll have to call a serviceman to work on the air conditioner."

"Still, that's pretty good! I'm sure that relieved her mind a great deal." Amy snuggled close to her husband on the couch as she thought about what had happened. "You didn't tell me you were going to propose that project."

Of course, Ted had told Amy about the group of salespeople, and had mentioned it would be fun to try a similar project in a neighborhood. But he hadn't planned this announcement. "I sensed they would be open to the idea," he explained. "It's a good mix of people. I think we'll all learn a lot."

"What do you expect to learn?" his wife asked.

"I would expect to confirm some things I've observed over the years about those who come closest to achieving their full potential. And I hope to learn some new ideas that will help me fulfill my own potential." Then he gazed at his wife and smiled. "And maybe, I can learn how to be a better husband and father."

"You're already pretty good!" Amy said.

"Well, thank you! But there's always room for improvement. If I'm going to achieve my potential, then I need to keep on learning. In fact, I need to start a notebook so I can record what we learn."

Ted went to his den and got an empty, spiral-bound, ruled notebook and labeled it "Fir Court Potential Project." On the first page he wrote:

POTENTIAL PROJECT

Over the next year, I want to interact with neighbors, and find ways we can achieve our potential better and enjoy life more.

Some of the areas we might examine are:
- Life planning
- Learning and growing
- Personal organization
- Time management
- Relating effectively with people
- Discovering and using our strengths
- Handling interruptions
- Following through
- Dealing with worry
- Learning to love what you have to do

He showed it to Amy. "In one sense this project will involve some work," he admitted. "but I sure stand to learn a lot because now at least ten people know about this — and their experience and knowledge are resources from which I can draw."

"But you also want to share what you learn with the neighborhood."

"That's right. That will also benefit me. As I try to distill what I've learned and what each of these people contributes, in the process of giving it back to them, I will grow. And hopefully, each of them will benefit a great deal too."

Before heading to bed, Amy checked her calendar with Ted so she could schedule an evening with the Appletons. Before drifting off to sleep, Ted thought about what he'd probably tell Clark. It was one of the most significant lessons he'd learned, a concept that had given direction to his life and made every day an exciting challenge. Everyone who had seen this concept found it an important key to a productive, fulfilling life.

NEIGHBORHOOD PORTRAIT

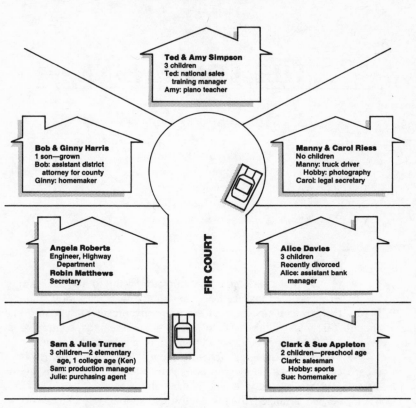

2

THE FINISH LINE

When Clark and Sue Appleton went to Ted and Amy's for dinner, Sue noted that the Simpsons' home was "elegantly simple." It was fine enough to entertain the company president, yet informal enough that kids didn't have to worry about breaking something at every turn. The living room was dominated by a baby grand piano.

"It's so nice outside," Ted told them, "that we decided to have a barbecue out back. Hope you don't mind steaks!" He led his guests through the sliding glass doors to the patio.

Sue had arranged for the Simpsons' junior high son to babysit so she didn't have to worry about the kids. "I think this is my first night away from the kids since we moved," she said. "I intend to enjoy it fully."

Though separated by more than ten years in age, the two couples had much in common. Both couples had married shortly after high school, so during dinner they swapped stories about their romances. Clark had been a salesman for several years and had some humorous experiences to swap with Ted. Amy related to Sue's life as a full-time mother with two preschool children. After teaching high school music for five years, Amy had decided to stay home and not work while the kids were small. "I realize not all women can do that," Amy acknowledged. "But I was fortunate that I was able to."

"I don't know how Alice does it," said Sue. "She has three kids to care for, plus a full-time job. I respect the fact that she is so disciplined, but I'm glad I don't have to do both."

After the dishes were cleared, Amy poured another round of iced tea. Ted asked Clark how he was doing in his business. "Really, pretty good," Clark answered. "I've improved each year. We don't have much savings and some months are pretty tight, but we could be a lot worse off."

"Do you like your work?"

"I love it. But . . . I don't quite know how to say this. I wonder if I'm missing something. I know I can certainly improve over what I'm doing now. And . . . I'm not sure if I want to keep selling sports equipment the rest of my life."

"What else would you like to do?"

"That's the problem. I don't know. I signed a pro baseball contract right out of high school. My dream was to play major league baseball, so I didn't think about much else. Unfortunately a .140 batting average in rookie league won't take you very far. I found myself out of baseball after a year. I needed a job. I started working at a sporting goods store, then I went with an equipment firm selling to schools. So here I am, almost ten years later."

"Clark, did you watch the last Olympics?"

"Clark saw almost every hour of it on television," Sue said, rolling her eyes.

"Did you ever see a runner line up at the start of a race, take off at the crack of the gun, then stop and try to locate the finish line?"

"Of course not. All runners know where they're going and they don't stop until they cross the finish line."

"That's exactly right. And we need to do the same thing. What's the point of sprinting through life without knowing where we're going?"

"OK, I follow you. You're talking about setting goals. I set sales goals every year."

"I figured you did. You wouldn't be as successful as you are if you didn't. But what about your life?"

"What do you mean?"

"Have you thought about where you'd like to be ten years from now? Or twenty years? Have you set any long-range objectives for yourself, your career, or your family?"

"I think about it once in a while. But no, I haven't really done that."

"Is the reasoning any different? How can you achieve your

potential if you don't even know where you're heading? It's just like a race. A runner must make every step count toward the goal if he wants to do his best. But he can't do that if he doesn't even know where the finish line is."

"It's a little like that slogan: 'Aim at nothing and you're sure to hit it,' " Amy added.

"I guess that makes sense," Clark admitted. "But how do you find the finish line? I can set sales goals, but how do I set objectives for my life if I don't know what I really want to do?"

"That's a good question. Why don't we move inside so I can show you something." Amy suggested that dessert be served in the living room. While she was dishing up homemade ice cream, Ted showed Clark and Sue a plaque that was hanging in his den:

MAKE THE MOST OF YOU

- **Y** OURSELF—Discover your strengths
- **O** BJECTIVES—Determine where you're going (your goals)
- **U** SE—Make good use of your strengths and your opportunities to reach your objectives

"This acrostic — YOU — helps me remember three very important principles. I need to know who I am — especially my strengths. I need to have clearly defined objectives or goals — both short-term and long-term. Then I need to take stock of the opportunities before me and make good use of them and my strengths to reach my objectives. It's a simple yet powerful concept."

"It sounds like something that could help anyone," Sue observed.

"Absolutely. It's true for anyone in any situation. Amy and I have both found this very helpful in her life. Why don't we move to the living room for dessert and we'll tell you more about it."

Since they all took time to enjoy the ice cream, it was a few minutes before they resumed the discussion. Ted started by saying, "While this concept is pretty simple, many people never stop to think about it. That's a major reason why so many people are unfulfilled. They sort of know that they aren't doing their best, and what is more enjoyable to them. But they don't know what to do about it.

"It probably would help if we got specific. Each one of us is unique. We each have certain God-given strengths. Clark, why don't you tell us some of your strengths."

"Well, I get along well with people." Clark was a little embarrassed because he didn't want to brag. "I'm pretty good with numbers . . ."

"He remembers every major league batting average since 1902," Sue joked.

"A statistics man!" laughed Ted. "Good. What else?"

Clark thought for a minute. "Are you looking for my skills?"

"Not just skills. Anything you consider a strength. Certainly that includes your talents. It also could be certain positive character qualities. Or certain circumstances that have made you what you are. Or people who've had an impact on your life. Would it help if I demonstrate?"

"I think it would."

"One of my strengths is that I am able to see the big picture in our company and instill that vision in our sales force. That is a skill I have. Another skill is my ability to observe a lot of information and note patterns or principles. For example, recently I led a brainstorming meeting about ways we could serve our sales force better. We probably had fifty ideas on the flip chart. I helped the group focus on *three* of the ideas which we could implement and gain a large percentage of the benefit we could have gained from *all* of the ideas.

"Now, here are certain facts about me that I also consider strengths. I have seventeen years of experience with one insurance company. I have a bachelor's degree from State University School of Business. I have a very talented wife who has strengths in areas where I'm weak. Those are important facts about me. Amy, what are some of your strengths?"

"Well, I guess I'd better say that one of my strengths is Ted!" Everyone laughed, and Sue noted how comfortable this couple was in their relationship. "I am gifted at playing the piano, and I'm able to teach people how to play the piano. While Ted has big dreams, I'm much more of a detail person. I tend to see all the little things that need to get done in order to reach a goal."

"That is so true!" Ted looked proudly at his wife as he added, "Sometimes I get a great idea, but it really isn't very practical. Amy, however, immediately sees some things that might make it work.

Without her input, that idea simply wouldn't happen. I didn't understand our differences when we were first married. I thought she was trying to squash my ideas because she'd always come up with reasons why something couldn't be done. Only in recent years have I realized she isn't trying to discourage me. It's just that she sees what is required to accomplish my 'big dreams.' I can benefit by knowing that information. That is why it's so important to know our strengths."

"And Ted helps me see the big picture," Amy added. "I used to think he wasn't very practical. He always had such grandiose ideas. But I needed to learn how to dream a little, to expand my horizons."

"So many couples fight over their differences," Ted concluded. "They don't realize that their differences are actually advantages."

Ted noted that Clark was leaning back in his chair, hand on chin, reflecting on what he'd heard. "Does this make sense?" Ted asked.

"Yes, it does. My problem is that I'm not sure I'm consciously aware of my strengths, and that can hurt me."

"It sure can. Also, we're not always the best judge of our own strengths and weaknesses. That's why there are tests available to help us learn that information. A few years ago my company had me take a test that helped me understand myself better. There are at least a dozen good tests I know of that measure such things as personality, communication style, vocational interests, and internal motivation. Many companies test their employees in order to utilize their personnel better."

"I think I had to take some sort of personality test when I was hired by my present employer," Clark remembered. "I never found out the results, but I understand we're allowed to examine our personnel files. Do you think I should do that?"

"You bet! In fact, my present job is the direct result of one important fact I discovered on my test. That's when I became aware that one of my great motivations in life is to help projects and people reach their full potential. I want to achieve my full potential, and I want those around me — my family, my fellow employees, my company — to achieve their full potential. That had always been true of me, but I wasn't aware of how much it motivated me. That information helped me clarify my objectives in the company, for that's when I realized I wanted to start learning how to train other salesmen rather than just selling insurance myself. Now, I'm not saying that I have the privilege of only doing what motivates me the most. That's not realistic to expect. But I am able to spend significant time in activities that match my strengths.

"Sue, we're not just talking about our jobs. This applies at home, as well. Would you like to tell us some of your strengths?"

"Well, I don't know," she answered, a blush creeping into her face. "I'm a decent mother . . . at least I hope I am. And I like to do things for people."

"That's true," Amy affirmed. "I thought it was great that you volunteered to help Alice last week."

"Sue's always doing that," Clark said. "She doesn't feel she's the leadership type, but she'll get in there and help. She's also a great listener. Everywhere we've lived, women seem to feel comfortable pouring out their troubles to her."

Ted was glad to see Clark praising his wife and pointed that out. "It's really important to let your wife know when you see a strength. She may not get the feedback you get in your work, so she needs to hear that from you. Maybe you and Sue can talk more about her strengths from time to time.

"Now that we've seen how discovering our strengths is so very important, let's talk about the second principle, determining objectives. Where do you want to go with your life?"

"I do have one goal," Clark said. "I'd like to lead our company in sales some day."

"Do you have that written down somewhere?"

"Well, no. It's in my head."

"OK, what about some other objectives? Where would you like to be with your career in ten years? How about your family? Do you have any goals for raising your children, or in your marriage?"

Clark thought for a moment. "I guess I don't. Well, nothing specific. Of course, I'd like my kids to turn out well. And as far as my career . . . I might like to move on to something else, but I don't have anything specific."

"There are two reasons for writing down your objectives. First, it forces you to make them more specific and measurable so you can see how you are doing. It's hard to measure progress toward a vague idea. But when you have it written down and there's a place where you can see it often, you tend to focus more on the objective. And that helps you set short-term and intermediate goals that move you closer to the finish line.

"For instance, instead of saying you'd like to lead the company in sales, you might say something like, 'within five years I want to have annual sales of a specific amount.' And instead of hoping your kids turn out OK, you might identify the qualities of life you want them to have when they leave the nest. By setting a clear finish line, it's then possible to see year by year how close you are to it.

"A second reason for written objectives is to be sure you include in your daily activities what you think is really significant in life. When you blow out the candles on your 80th birthday cake what would you like to look back and see has been accomplished? What do you value greatly? What greatly burdens or motivates you?"

Amy illustrated determining objectives for their family. "For our oldest, Nancy, as we saw her develop, we started thinking that going to college made sense for her. In light of that, we encouraged her to take some accelerated courses in high school. This year one of our goals that relates to our overall objective is to help her select a college by Christmas. Our son, as you know, has started baby sitting. We're using this to teach him how to be a conscientious worker and how to handle money, which are things we'd like all of our children to know when they leave home."

Ted opened his wallet and pulled out a well-worn 3 x 5 card. "I keep my life objectives on this little card and I look at it at least once a week. One of my life-long objectives is 'to help a maximum number of people achieve their God-given potential.' In light of that objective, I have a ten-year goal to be a consultant to companies, helping them help their personnel achieve their potential. A five-year goal is to complete my masters in business administration, with specialization in human resource development. I also have family and other goals and objectives. Amy told you how we set goals for teaching our kids. When they reach the age of eighteen, we want them to be independent and to know what is really important in life."

"Wow, you guys are really organized!" Sue observed.

"I like your system," Clark added. "By the way, there's one thing I do with my sales goals. I keep them taped to the dash of my car so I see them every day."

"That's a good idea," said Ted. "I do a similar thing by keeping some of my objectives on a 3 x 5 card on my desk at work. I have another one on my bathroom mirror."

Clark reviewed what he'd learned so far. "OK, Ted, I can see that I need to discover my strengths. And I need to determine my objectives. What about that third principle of using my strengths and opportunities to reach my objectives?"

"In my work goals, did you notice how my plans matched my strengths?" Ted elaborated: "I know some people who are well aware of their strengths. But they don't have clearly defined objectives. And there are others who have big dreams, but those dreams aren't realistic because they don't line up with their strengths and skills. As a result, they often don't differentiate well between strategic opportunities which offer a good match of strength and objective and unstrategic opportunities which don't."

Clark laughed. "That's the truth! Ever since I was a little kid I dreamed of being a major league baseball player. I did real well in Little League and high school. But when I made the jump to the professional level, it became obvious that I'd never make it to the top. No matter how hard I worked, I simply didn't have the physical ability."

"So you see the point! By discovering our strengths and determining our objectives, we now have the two ingredients that, when combined with our specific opportunities and circumstances, help us achieve our full potential. And we are not just more productive; we are much more satisfied because our daily activities tend more to be things we are good at and enjoy doing. What's more, we have the deep satisfaction of contributing toward what we think is of importance and long-term value.

"Now, granted, we won't get a perfect match. We can't always do just the things we like doing and that are our strengths. But certainly, moving in a positive direction is better than having no idea where to go.

"Let me illustrate. When I realized that I had a strength in motivating people and helping them achieve their potential, that affected my approach to specific selling opportunities. I always believed in my product, but I actually began selling more by learning my customers' goals and showing them how they could move closer to their goals with my product. Occasionally when my product didn't fit their needs, I said so and even recommended where they might go to get what they needed. People really appreciated that.

"I also expanded my vision and started thinking about how I could use my strength in broader ways. Instead of just selling, I could work with other salesmen. So that became an objective, to become a sales manager. Then I started thinking of how I might help even more people, and two years ago I proposed the job of national training director to the company. Last year they created the position and promoted me to fill it.

"And it isn't like I am always making opportunities happen. Sometimes they 'just happen' and now I recognize them better. For example, our biggest customer called the president of our company one day and said they desperately needed help in training their sales force. The president asked me if I would take a month off from my regular job and consult and train the customer's people. I quickly recognized that this was a wonderful way for me to organize my thoughts better and be stretched to apply them in a fresh setting. It was a step toward achieving my potential. Before I understood about my strengths and objectives, I might have rejected the opportunity.

"So in the past ten years I've become more productive and more fulfilled. If I hadn't discovered this strength, I might still be selling today. I'd have just a fraction of the internal motivation and I'd have fulfilled just a fraction of my potential.

"The same is true with my family. When I started thinking

about how I could help my wife and children achieve their potential, I actually started enjoying them more. Amy is a very talented musician and I wanted to see her use her abilities to their fullest. Honey, why don't you tell Clark and Sue what you did."

Amy leaned forward in her chair. "As you know, I taught music at the high school level. I believe I was a good teacher, but I discovered that I was much more effective teaching one-on-one than to a class. I simply wasn't that skilled in managing a large group. But I had great results when I worked with students individually. In addition, much of my job was leading a choir, yet my strength and interest was piano. When we had our first child, it was easy to stop teaching school. I knew I wanted to resume teaching when the kids got older, but I really didn't want to go back to the classroom. That's when the idea of teaching piano in my home emerged. Just after that a friend approached me about tutoring her two children in piano. I recognized that as a good opportunity to start. Now I'm teaching a number of children three afternoons a week. And someday, when the kids are grown, I plan to make it a full-time business."

"Do you also keep your goals on 3 x 5 cards?" asked Sue.

Amy laughed. "Ted has suggested that, but it's not very helpful to me. Let me show you what I did." She rose and led her guests to the kitchen. There by the phone was a small cork board, and in one corner she had a neatly printed sheet which followed the YOU outline. She had listed some of her strengths, some long-range objectives, and some activities that would match her strengths and objectives.

"Let me show you how this works. As I said, one of my strengths is observing detail, and I've written that down. One of my current opportunities is that I am a mother of three children still at home. One of my long-range objectives is to raise children who are prepared to stand on their own when they're eighteen years old. How do I match those? Well, there are many things I can do. One activity I'm working on presently is a notebook for each of my three children. In that notebook, I'm putting family photographs from over the years, and writing down memorable lessons we've learned together. This is something each of my children will take with him when he leaves home."

"What a great idea!" Sue said. "I like the way you've thought this through. You know, I've thought about getting involved in some community activities, but I haven't gotten specific. This gives me a way to get started."

Amy asked if anyone wanted seconds on ice cream. Clark and Ted eagerly accepted. Back in the living room, Ted picked up again on the importance of the third principle — *Use*. "Once we know our *strengths*, and have clearly defined *objectives*, it's important to develop a plan that *uses* those strengths to help us reach our objectives. Again, realize that we won't get a perfect match, but we can aim in that direction. That's what Amy was just showing you. We're always refining the process. When I first discovered that my strength was helping people reach their potential, I didn't really know the specifics of that strength. That's why I decided to start a notebook, and I challenged several of my fellow salesmen to work with me. We agreed to meet once a week for breakfast to discuss ways we could reach our potential. We all learned a lot through that process."

"Sounds familiar!" Sue smiled. "That explains why you made the offer at our block party. It was a new opportunity to match your strengths and objectives."

"That's right. Ted's always looking for learning opportunities," Amy said. "In fact, we learn together, and it's our desire to continue to learn for the rest of our lives. That's one reason life is so much fun. How many notebooks have you filled, Ted?"

"Three. I'm starting a fourth one with this neighborhood project. But I'm always trying to simplify it into a few basic, universal principles. The *YOU* outline became one of the first major simplified outlines — and one of the most useful. It came out of that weekly meeting with the salesmen."

As Clark was scooping up the final bite of ice cream, he observed, "You know, there's something sad about a person who has talent, but no direction. Sue, you remember old George."

Sue and Clark had met in high school, and George was a classmate who succeeded at everything he tried. He was a star athlete, active in school politics, a bright student. "I ran into him the other day. He dropped out of college because he didn't know what he wanted to do. He's bounced around from job to job. He's got all that ability, but he's never figured out what he wants to do with his life. So he's unproductive and unfulfilled. He certainly hasn't come close to achieving his potential."

"I think we all know people like that," Ted added. "It's tragic. But we don't have to let that happen to us. We may not have the talent to be great athletes or musicians. But we all have abilities, and I believe we have a responsibility to recognize our talents and do all we can to use them well."

"You've convinced me," Clark said. "In the next few days I am going to sit down and think through what my strengths are. Then I'd like to try to write out an objective statement. Then I'll see if I can come up with one or two activities that match my strengths and objectives. Would you mind looking it over in a couple of weeks, just to see if I've defined it enough?"

Ted was proud to see his friend eager to make use of what he had just learned. "I'd be glad to do that. By the way, I have some extra copies of the *YOU* acrostic. Would you like one?"

"I sure would!"

Ted got them the copy. As the Appletons prepared to leave, Clark suddenly remembered an idea he'd wanted to propose. "You know that vacant lot behind our house? A certain amount of the land in this development is supposed to be green belt. I know there are plans for some playgrounds and parks in this area. I was wondering what the plans are for that lot. There's no 'For Sale' sign. Maybe we could make a play area there: a basketball court, some swings for the kids. I think there's city money available if the neighbors help do some of the work."

"That's a good idea," Ted answered. "I'm involved in the neighborhood association, so I might be able to check in City Hall and see what they've got planned. I wonder if Sam would also be interested in that. Why don't we talk with him and see what we can organize."

Clark liked that idea, and mentioned that he'd also noticed how organized Sam was. "I was in his home the other day; I've never seen anyone's desk so neat. Maybe he could tell me how I can get better organized."

"I could use some help myself in that area," Ted admitted. "Let's get in touch with Sam next week."

*Some practical ways to gain
control of your schedule and
organize your home and office.*

3

TIME TO GET
ORGANIZED

Clark, Sam, and Ted were playing a game of "cut-throat" pool in Sam's basement. Earlier they had spent some time looking over the open lot, discussing ways a playground might be organized. Ted had learned the property was available for park development and had agreed to circulate a petition to determine support for a neighborhood participation project. Now the three were relaxing with a fun game.

Well, maybe relaxing wasn't the right word for Sam. He never did anything halfheartedly. He carefully studied each shot and systematically racked up points, often sinking five or more shots in a row. Clark managed to keep things interesting, both competitively and with his lively patter. Ted simply enjoyed the show and the occasional easy shots he was able to make.

Clark had a perfect set-up to make a run at Sam. His first shot was straight on, but he missed it and wound up leaving the six-ball on the lip. Sam moved in for the kill, ready to end the game. Clark laughed at his mistake and looked knowingly at Ted. "Guess shooting pool isn't one of my strengths!"

"Were you able to make a list of your strengths?" asked Ted.

"Yes, I was. In fact, I was able to look over my personnel file at work. It confirmed some things I already knew. For example, that I'm personable, and I do not hide my feelings. I was surprised to find that I rated very high in being impulsive. I thought I was more disciplined."

"Did you write out some objectives?"

"I sure did! I wrote out two long-range objectives for my work on a 3 x 5 card and taped it to the dash of my car. I really appreciate the help you gave me."

"Would you care to share your objectives with me?"

"I'd like to be the company's top salesman within the next three years. I've calculated how much more business I'd have to generate to reach that goal, and the potential contacts I have for more sales. Realistically, I think I can do it. My second objective is to become an expert on safety in sports equipment. That will help me better serve my clients and it's an interest I have from my own sports background. I don't know why I didn't think about setting long-range goals before. They sure help give me direction."

"Do you have any specific activities to help you move toward either of those objectives?"

"One of my short-term goals is to increase my percentage of repeat business. So I'm planning to make some additional calls in the next three months to schools that bought equipment from me last spring."

"Did you set any family objectives?"

"Oh yeah, I forgot. I need to do that. It's probably a good idea to do that with Sue, wouldn't you say?"

"Very important. You could also encourage her to discover some of her strengths."

"I'll take her out to dinner next week. Maybe we can set some goals together as a couple."

"Would you guys cut the chatter?" Sam asked as he lined up a shot. There was quiet for a moment as he tallied two more points. As he set up a new rack, he asked, "Now, what were you guys jabbering about?"

Clark explained the *YOU* outline and Sam grunted his approval as he prepared to break. "OK, three more balls and this game is history."

As Sam put away the winning shot, he observed, "You really are serious about that project you proposed at the block party. I mean, you really want to learn how to achieve your potential."

"Absolutely!" said Ted. "I don't want simply to fill my days with activities. I know I can't do everything, but I can accomplish a great deal if I have a plan. The *YOU* approach is simple. Identify my strengths. Know where I want to go. Then match the two. That way I'll be highly motivated and I'll be well on my way to achieving my maximum potential."

Sam leaned against the pool table and reflected on those words. "What do you do when you're stuck in a job you don't like?" He had worked for years in a food processing and packaging plant, beginning as an equipment operator and working his way up to his present position as production manager.

"What's wrong with your job?" Clark asked.

"Maybe I should clarify that. There are parts of my job that I enjoy. But I'm stuck in my position. I've gone as far as I can in the company. It's a family-owned operation and there's no way I'll have any more responsibility. I'm just not excited about staying in this job for another fifteen or twenty years. The people who work under me aren't very motivated and sometimes I get so frustrated trying to get them to stay on top of production. And a couple of the people above me are real pains to work with."

"Why don't you quit? Get a job somewhere else."

"I've thought about it. But the job pays well. And I've got a wife and two young kids to consider, so I can't just walk away from the benefits."

"What would you really like to do if you had your choice?" Ted asked.

Sam smiled and hung up his pool cue. "Let me show you!" He opened the door of the game room into a carpentry shop that took up half of his garage. "Here she is, my pride and joy!"

It was a fully-equipped shop. A workbench ran the length of one wall. Above it, all neatly grouped according to category, were handsaws, chisels, planes, drills and awls, hammers, screwdrivers, files and rasps, wrenches, pliers, various levels, squares and measures, plus a number of small power tools. In the middle of the room was a table saw and on the opposite wall hung several blades for the saw. In one corner were a drill press and lathe, and, like the table saw, both were mounted on braked casters for mobility.

Suddenly, a flash of anger crossed Sam's face as he noticed a pile of sawdust on the floor by the table saw, plus several tools and some nails lying on the work bench. "That stupid son of mine. I can't get him to clean up and put things away."

"This is the neatest shop I've ever seen!" Clark extolled.

"No kidding. I've never seen one so well-kept," Ted agreed. "Mine's nothing compared to this, but I still have a hard time keeping things in place. Seems like every month or so I'm looking all over the house for a hammer or screwdriver I left somewhere."

Clark noted a cabinet Sam was making from oak. "These are

beautiful. Do you sell them?"

"Most of the things I make are for my own use. I've made things for a few friends; I usually charge only to cover the cost of materials."

"I've seen work like this at shows and art fairs," said Ted. "With your quality you could sell a lot."

"Several people have told me that. I've thought about how much fun it would be to do that for a living, but I'm not ready to give up my steady income."

"What if you did just one or two shows a year and built up your business slowly. Then maybe in a few years you could make a living at it."

Sam thought about that as he replaced the tools his son Ken had left on the workbench. "I'll have to give that some consideration."

The men heard Julie come down the stairs and yell, "I've got some iced tea and chocolate chip cookies." The group moved back into the game room and as they eagerly attacked the refreshments, Sam asked Julie if the kids were in bed.

"Yes, no thanks to you!" Julie snapped. "Sometimes I think if they get out of bed and ask for another drink of water I'm going to tie them to their beds and gag them."

Sam ignored the putdown and the topic quickly changed as Ted noticed a couple of certificates honoring Julie for various community activities. "You've been involved with Scouts for several years," he observed.

"That's an important part of our kids' lives. Yes, I'm very involved."

"We've thought that our youngest child might be ready for that kind of thing."

"Why doesn't he come with me next week and see if he likes it?"

Clark observed the roll-top desk that occupied one corner of the room. "Hey, Sam! Did you make this? What a beauty. Mind if I open it?"

"Go ahead."

Clark carefully rolled open the top and noted the slots containing bills, receipts and letters. "This desk is so neat! Looks like you've got everything organized. Do you ever do any work here?"

"As a matter of fact, I do a lot of work at that desk."

"You ought to see my desk. I could use a roll top just to cover the mess. I don't think I've seen the top of it since two days after we moved into the house. Got piles of bills, order forms, product catalogs . . . you name it, it's somewhere in there."

"I'll bet you don't get things done as quickly and efficiently as you'd like," Sam said.

"Yeah, last month I was late paying an important bill just because I had it in the wrong place."

Ted saw an opportunity: "Would you mind telling us a little about your system? I won't say my desk is a disaster, but I sure could improve."

"It's a very simple system, really," Sam said. "You'll notice the calendar." It was the one item lying on his desk top. "This is my schedule book. It goes everywhere with me."

Month AUGUST **19____**

SUN	MON	TUE	WED	THU	FRI	SAT
/	/	/	1/ 18:00 MANAGER'S MEETING 4:00 PLANT TOUR	2/ 11:30-1:30 FAREWELL LUNCHEON FOR GAIL	3/ 2:30-4:00 POLICY REVIEW COMMITTEE	4/ 1:15 BALL GAME
5/	6/ 7:00 - BUILD SHELVES FOR BATHROOM	7/	8/ 10:00 MANAGER'S MEETING 4:00 PLANT TOUR 7:00 MEETING W/CLARK & TED	9/ 7:00 - THINK ABOUT COMPUTERIZED PRODUCTION PROPOSAL	10/ SIMPSON JOB MUST BE COMPLETED - CALL GEORGE	11/ JULIE'S FRIEND OVER FOR VISIT
12/	13/ 8:00 - DROP CAR OFF FOR TUNE-UP	14/ CRANDALL JOB MUST BE COMPLETED - CALL ALL	15/ 10:00 - MANAGER'S MEETING 4:00 PLANT TOUR	16/ 10:00 - 12:00 PRODUCTION METHODS TRAINING SESSION 3:00 - 5:00 DENTIST APPOINTMENT	17/ DEVELOPMENT REVIEWS DUE	18/ PUT FERTILIZER & WEED KILLER ON LAWN
19/		21/		23/		

Clark noted that Sam had even written down their visit that evening. "Seems like you have something going all the time."

"I'll say," Julie cracked. "I hardly ever see him except at dinner. And after work, he spends most of his time in that shop."

Sam gave his wife a quick, sharp glance, then continued talking as though nothing had happened. "I've seen a lot of different systems. But basically, I need one place where I can record my appointments and other commitments or deadlines. Each morning I check this first thing so I know what's up for the day."

"Mind if I look through this a minute?" Clark asked. Sam nodded and Clark flipped through the book. "I need something more detailed because of my sales calls. I keep a daily appointment book in my car."

"There are plenty of options. I use a monthly calendar, but you could use a weekly, or daily, depending on what you need. There's enough space on mine to note several appointments each day."

"You have both work and personal appointments on your calendar. Why do you do that? I don't mix the two."

"Why not have everything in one place?"

"I guess that makes some sense. Hey, what's this?" Clark noted a page in the front of Sam's schedule book:

STANDARD DAILY SCHEDULE

5:00	Rise, exercise, shower
6:00	Breakfast at Cook's Cafe
	Dictation
8:00	Arrive at office,
	phone calls
10:00	Priority project
12:00	Lunch
1:00-5:00	Meetings
6:00	Home, dinner
7:00	Shop

"Oh, that's the way I try to spend my day."

"Why do you have your meetings in the afternoon?"

"I find that I'm not as productive by myself after lunch. Since I have to have meetings — they're a fact of life in my job — and since I'm more efficient in the afternoons when I work with others, that's when I try to schedule most meetings. In the morning when I'm more alert, I prefer to work alone when I can."

"Looks like you're a morning person," Ted observed.

Julie laughed at that. "That's the truth. Often he's up and working before the rest of us know what's happened."

"I'm sharpest in the morning," Sam agreed. "So I try to arrange my schedule so I can get a lot done then. I realize that doesn't work for everyone. If I were more alert in the evenings, I'd arrange my day differently."

"What do you do at the cafe?" asked Ted.

"I drink my coffee, scan the newspaper, and eat breakfast. Then I do some of my dictation, so I have work for my secretary as soon as I arrive at the office. Then I get phone calls out of the way. That way I can leave messages if someone's not available. By 10:00 I've gotten a lot done. I try to do a major project from then until noon. Maybe it's working on a problem in the plant, or studying production plans for a new line. I usually have my secretary hold my calls during that time."

"You follow this every day?" Clark asked, unable to believe someone could be so structured.

Sam laughed. "No, I'm lucky to have a day like that once a week. But it's my ideal. I find this works best for me, so it makes sense to try to follow it as much as possible."

Ted asked Julie if she followed a similar plan.

"Yes, Sam's taught me a lot about being personally organized and getting the most out of my day. I've got a job that allows me to work flexible hours. I have to get the kids off to school, or now, their summer day camp activities. We're part of a car pool. On days I drive, I'm in the office by 9:00. The other days, it's 8:30."

"What do you do?"

"I'm a purchasing agent. Like my husband, there's a normal pattern to my day. Usually I have a pile of requisitions on my desk when I arrive. I sort them, then spend most of the morning on the phone with vendors. Then in the afternoon, I do the paper work. Once a week I leave at 3:00 for Scouts. Otherwise I'm usually through by 4:00 or 4:30. I pick up the kids, come home and fix dinner. Then evenings, I've often got activities with the kids, whether its sports or some school project."

"This is great," Clark said. "I wish there were some pattern to my life. I have appointments scattered throughout the day. Sometimes there's three or four hours between calls."

"How do you use that time?" asked Ted.

"Oh, play a round of golf!" Clark quipped. "Well, sometimes I do. But actually, I'll go to a coffee shop. Maybe I'll make a couple of phone calls."

"Do you have any paperwork?"

"Sure — I have to write up the orders."

"When do you do that?"

"Usually at night; I bring them home. But many times I'm tired and I don't feel like doing them, so sometimes I'll save them for the next day."

"I'll bet we could find a way to help you get better use of your time."

"My wife wouldn't mind," Clark laughed. "She wishes I wouldn't bring work home."

"Why don't you do your paperwork as soon as you finish an appointment? That is if you don't have another one scheduled immediately. Then it's out of the way."

"I should. It's just that I don't like doing it. And I get so involved in my appointments that I like to unwind a bit."

"There's nothing wrong with taking a few minutes to unwind. But do you need two hours?"

"Not really. I could take a few minutes to relax, then write up the order. Of course, some of my appointments are after school and so I usually come right home after that. Sometimes it's a couple of days before I get to those."

"But if you wrote up the earlier orders during the dead time, you'd have more time at home for your family. Is that right?"

"Yes, I need to do that."

"You might consider doing the rest of your paperwork before your first call in the morning. Then it's not hanging over your head. And if you really don't like doing it, you've gotten your most unpleasant task out of the way first. The rest of the day is bound to be more enjoyable."

"May I make an observation?" Sam asked. "What you've done is illustrate the importance of priorities. Did you ever hear the story about the time management consultant who was talking to a company president who felt his employees weren't reaching their potential? The consultant said he had one recommendation, and this was it: Always start with your top-priority project, and continue doing it until it's finished before moving on to the next priority. The consultant told the president to try it and then pay whatever he thought it was worth. A few weeks later, the company sent the consultant a check for $25,000."

Sam chuckled as he thought for a moment. "Unfortunately, I wasn't that consultant. But if you'd like to make a donation to a worthy cause, well, I wouldn't refuse your offer!"

Ted and Clark laughed at Sam's humor. Then Ted noted, "You've really made the point that we may not get everything done in a day. But by always doing our top priorities, we know we'll get the most important things done."

"Does that mean I never take a break?" asked Clark.

Sam answered. "No, we all need to take breaks. And when we do, that becomes top priority. But often we waste time because we don't think about our priorities. One thing that keeps me from wasting too much time is a *'To Do List.'* Let me show you." Sam took his schedule book and turned to the back page and showed Clark and Ted:

STATUS	PRIORITY	TO DO LIST
		WEDNESDAY
✓	6	SCHEDULE WILLIAMS JOB
✓	7	" ADAMS "
✓	4	" FORNEY "
	13	" RALPH'S "
✓	2	CHECK ON SIMPSON "
✓	8	" " TORRANCE "
✓	3	" " CRANDALL "
	9	" " SORENSON "
✓	1	ATTEND TODAY'S MANAGER'S MEETING
	11	PREPARE FOR THE PRODUCTION METHODS
		TRAINING SESSION NEXT WEEK
✓	5	TOUR PLANT
	12	COMPLETE DEVELOPMENTAL REVIEWS
		DUE BY END OF NEXT WEEK
	10	REVIEW MONTHLY BUDGET REPORT

"You'll notice that I have a lot of things on my list, but I've numbered them according to their priority. During the day I try to work on my highest priority item until it's done. Then I check it off and move on to the next priority until it's done."

Ted had an observation. "Sam, one thing I've found in prioritizing is that I need to distinguish between that which is *important* and that which is *urgent*. If all we do is take care of the urgent — the emergencies — we often don't get the important things done. I like your schedule because it allows you time to do those truly priority things that will move you forward toward your objectives."

Clark was impressed with the order he'd seen in Sam's schedule. He looked again at the desk, noted the slots, and wondered, "Sam, I hope you don't mind my asking, but how do you stay on top of all your paperwork? I mean, I don't see any piles."

"A place for everything and everything in its place," said Sam. "It's an old saying, but true. I don't like clutter. I find it takes very little time to put everything in a cubby hole or a file folder. Over the years, it's become a habit. Rather than putting something down in a pile and sorting it later, I do it immediately."

Sam opened a file drawer in the desk to illustrate his system. Clark noted file labels such as:

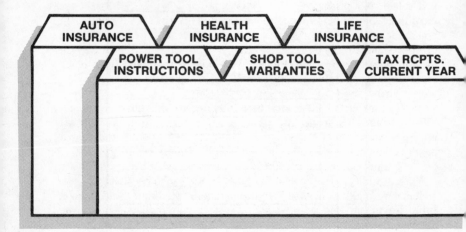

"Seems like this would take a lot of time," said Clark.

"How much time does it take you to find a warranty?" asked Sam.

Clark blushed as he admitted, "You win. Sometimes I can spend an hour or more looking for something."

"So why not invest a little time up front? In the long run I save hours trying to find things."

"Sam's taught me a lot in this area," Julie interjected. "His personal organization is one thing that attracted me to him initially. I have a similar file system upstairs. There's a little desk by the kitchen phone where I keep files for all the household appliances, coupons, and so on."

"One thing I couldn't stand when the kids were younger was

toys strewn all over the house. Julie got a bunch of plastic tubs. She had all the toys categorized and she taught the kids to pick up the toys and put them in the tubs at the end of each day."

"You can buy the tubs for a dollar or two, depending on the size," Julie explained. "I use them now to organize my closets. I have one for my sewing patterns, several for fabrics. I put our pharmaceuticals in one, and so on."

"Could my wife see your system sometime?" Ted asked. "She's been trying to find a better way to organize our closets."

"I've been trying to get Ken to learn this," Sam said. "Sometimes we just shut off his room so we don't have to look at it."

Ted had listened intently to the discussion and asked if he could summarize what he'd learned this evening. "Sam, I believe I've heard you relate four principles. First, it's important to have a system for recording your appointments and commitments right away, and then you refer to that schedule often. Second, you need to have an idea of your standard day or week. Third, you prioritize activities and do the top priority item first. Finally, you said there should be a place for everything and everything should be in its place."

"That's about it," Sam agreed.

"I'm going to clear my desk this weekend," Clark resolved. "You're right. It's worth my time to get a better filing system set up. Hey, Sam, could I pay you to build an organizer for the top of my desk, so I could have a place for my mail, bills, and so forth?"

"I think so. Let me take a look and see what I can do."

Ted and Clark thanked the Turners for the time that evening. "I feel I've really benefited," Ted remarked at the door. "And thanks, Julie, for the invitation to Scouts. I'll have Amy call you about the details."

"I've really enjoyed this," Sam said. Then, soberly, he added, "I kind of envy you guys."

"Why do you say that?" Ted asked. "We really admire your organization."

"Sure, I'm organized. But you two obviously like your work, and you probably enjoy the people you work with. I don't have either."

Ted realized this was a rare confession for Sam, who obviously had succeeded partly because of his outstanding organizational ability. "Maybe we can talk about it some time," he said.

"I'd like that," he said. Then he looked at his watch. "Well, I'd better hit the sack. Five o'clock comes pretty early. Hey, I really enjoyed it. Let's get together again sometime."

At home, Ted wrote about the evening in his notebook. He thought about the four principles he'd observed in Sam, and after playing with some letters, wrote down the following:

MANAGE YOUR TIME

- **N** OTE commitments right away
- **A** RRANGE your standard day
  or week
- **P** UT everything in its place
- **S** TART and finish top priorities first

"How about that!" Ted said to himself. *"NAPS!* If I were as organized as Sam, I'd have time to take naps. Or do some additional reading. Or spend more time with the kids."

He thought for a moment and realized that he was doing a pretty good job with recording his commitments, arranging his standard schedule, and doing priority activities first. But he could use a better system for organizing his desk. He pulled out his calendar and wrote in the space for the following Saturday: "Clean den. Clear desk. Put all papers in files. Store files in file cabinet."

Then he thought some more about how he had both a calendar for family commitments and a date book for his business. "I wonder," he thought, "if I should combine my calendars so that all my commitments — family and business — are in one place."

Before he turned off the light and headed for bed, Ted thought of Sam's final comments. Sam really was organized, but he didn't have the people skills Clark had. And that was hindering his effectiveness as a person. Clark and several others in the neighborhood seemed to have succeeded, at least in part, because they worked well with people. Was there some way the neighbors could help him?

Caring for people, listening to them and affirming them — three ways to more effective, enjoyable relationships.

4

RELATING TO PEOPLE

It was a gorgeous fall day, the kind on which you don't mind working outside. Everyone except Bob and Ginny turned out for the neighborhood work party. The city had approved the open lot behind the Appletons for use as a playground and had provided funding for equipment if the neighbors would install it. Angela, Clark and Sam were assembling the equipment while Ken, Manny and Ted dug holes for several large posts.

They were ready to lift the swing set into its holes when the group stopped for lunch. Sue had prepared a large plate of cold cuts and bread while several other women provided salads and dessert.

As plates of cookies and brownies circled the two adjoining picnic tables, Ted asked for everyone's attention. "Two months ago, I proposed a project in which we as a neighborhood would exchange ideas with each other about how to achieve our potential. I'd like to make my first report to you."

Alice was eager to hear the report. "Ever since several of you helped me get settled into my new home, I've been intrigued by this project."

"Well, we've just started," Ted continued. Briefly he told about the evenings with the Appletons and the Turners. "I've distilled what we've learned so far into two acrostics. The first is *YOU* — make the most of YOU. *'Y'* stands for *Yourself: Discovering your strengths.* *'O'* stands for *Objectives: Determine where you're going — your* goals. And *'U'* stands for *Use: Make good use of your strengths and opportunities to reach your objectives."*

"What fun!" said Angela. "That's really practical, and easy to remember."

"That's the idea. This isn't an exercise in theory. We want to discover practical ways in which we can achieve our potential and enjoy life. Clark and Sue, maybe you could tell us how you've applied this lesson so far."

"After our evening together, I set some personal goals," Sue began. "I keep them on my cork board by the kitchen phone where I can see them several times each day. For example, I think one of my strengths is that I communicate well with little children. I've written down certain character qualities I want to build in my own kids — that's an objective in light of the opportunity of being a mother. In order to learn how to do that, I've bought and read a couple of books. I'm also thinking about taking a course at the community college that would help me understand children better. In fact, I've thought that someday when my kids are older, I might enjoy teaching in a pre-school program. So the course would give me some more input."

"Recognizing my strengths has really helped me," said Clark. "I'm a people person, but I'm not very good at details. I just don't like sitting in an office and doing paperwork. I guess that's confirmed why I like my job, and now I really want to be the best salesman I can possibly be. I'm starting to study more about it and my company is going to let me take a special seminar next month."

"I think the idea of knowing your strengths and setting goals relates to where my husband is at," said Carol.

Everyone looked at Manny. "That's right," he said as he fiddled with his camera. He'd already shot a roll during the morning, catching some unusual poses and expressions. "I've often thought about being a professional photographer, but I don't have any plan to get there. I'm going to have to think about how to do that."

"I can testify that you take great pictures," said Sue. "Your wife showed me some of your photos. I especially like the one that won a blue ribbon at the state fair."

Ted summarized the first point. "So we've seen that if we want to maximize our potential, we need to know who we are and where we are going and how those fit together. A second topic several of us have learned about is how to get better organized."

"Want to see Clark's desk?" Sue asked.

"It doesn't look like Sam's yet, but I'm making progress," Clark said. "Sam built an organizer for the top of my desk, so now it's much easier to find things. And Ted, I've even got time to take an occasional nap."

Ted had told Clark and Sam of his acrostic. "Sam thought that was clever," said Julie. "Why don't you tell everyone?"

"*NAPS* stands for four things we learned from Sam about organization," Ted explained. " '*N*' reminds us to *Note commitments right away;* '*A*' means *Arrange your standard day or week;* '*P*' tells us to *Put everything in its place;* and '*S*' means *Start and finish top priorities first.* Sam, you helped me by showing me some helpful systems. For instance, I've improved my process for sorting the mail. I'm forcing myself to handle everything just once whenever possible."

"I bought Ted some wire baskets for his desk," Amy explained. "He has one for bills, another for receipts, another for letters he needs to answer, and so on. Because he's more organized, he's able to spend more time on his pet projects."

"I sure wouldn't mind learning more about your systems," Alice sighed. "People think I'm so organized, but I feel overloaded. I sure could improve my scheduling and organization."

"Then you need to see Sam and Julie's place," Clark said.

"Please do come over some evening," Julie invited.

Sam now brought up the matter that had troubled him earlier. "If we're talking about reaching our potential, I wish you'd tell me how to deal with people who don't cooperate with your objectives. I mean, I think I know my strengths. I set goals, and I'm organized. But sometimes people louse up my plans. I'm thinking particularly of our head of marketing who thinks he knows all about production. He's always making unrealistic demands. He drives me crazy."

"If the rest of you don't mind, let's examine Sam's situation for a moment," said Ted. "Does anyone else have problems working with certain people?"

"You bet!" said Manny. "If you've ever been late with an important shipment, you sure can get an earful."

"I have three different bosses," added Carol, who worked in a law office. "Each one of them has a different style."

Angela and Alice also had occasional personality clashes with their bosses. "But the problem is not just at work," Alice observed. "I mean, sometimes I wonder where my teenage daughter's head is. She can drive me up the wall."

"So here are the guidelines for our discussion," said Ted. "We all want to achieve our potential, but we can't do it in a vacuum. It requires working with other people, whether at work, at home, in the neighborhood . . . whatever. Anyone have any ideas?"

There was a moment of silence while people thought about the situation. Then Clark jumped in. "Since I was with Sam the first time he mentioned his problem, I've given it some thought. One thing that works for me is that I try to get involved with each of my customers. I take an interest in them as people. Maybe that's easy for me because I do a lot of work with coaches and I have a sports background. I always like to find out how the coach's team is doing. Right now, football season is starting. When I visit a school, I don't just check to make sure they have all the equipment they need. I also ask how practice is going, and what their prospects are for the year. Sometimes I'll even go and see one of the games or practices. I think most of the coaches appreciate that."

Amy had similar experience with her piano students. "I think it's important that I look at them as more than just customers. I have to want them to succeed. Sometimes that means going the extra mile. I'll never forget my first piano teacher. She saw potential in me and she'd invite me to her home to practice on her grand piano. She'd let me listen to her recordings and borrow her music books. That was over and above what my parents paid for lessons. She didn't need to do that, but I know it made a significant difference in my life."

"Amy, you've shown me that in the way you've taken me under your wing," said Carol. "Just this morning I was feeling so nauseous and you spent a few minutes telling me how you got through morning sickness."

"Wait a minute — is this an announcement?" Sue wanted to know.

Carol beamed as she told her friends, "We just found out yesterday. We're expecting our first child next April."

Hearty congratulations came from around the table. Alice, Carol's neighbor to the south, put her hand on Carol's arm. "I'm really happy for you. Please let me know if there's anything I can do to help."

Robin, Angela's roommate, was the shiest person in this group. But she couldn't help noticing an important point during the last few minutes. "I think there's a word that describes what we've been talking about. It's *caring*. That is what Alice just did for Carol. That's what Clark is doing with his clients. That's what Amy was talking about with her piano teacher. And isn't that what we're seeing in our neighborhood? We get along because we care about each other."

"I think Robin's right," Alice agreed. "We're saying the other person is important and worth spending time with. Unfortunately, I think that's why I'm divorced. My former husband never considered his family important."

Julie picked up on that. "I think there's more to it than just being interested or caring, though that's a very important starting point. But for important relationships, there has to be more than just a casual 'how are you doing?' Whether it's my husband or someone at work, I want to know that they understand what I feel and think. Sometimes that takes time."

Sam gave his wife a nasty glance, but she ignored him. Ted noticed the non-verbal interplay and opened the subject up to the group. "What do the rest of you think?"

"I can tell you how important listening is," said Carol. "When Manny proposed, I didn't think we were ready to get married. But he was so enthusiastic and I didn't want to hurt him, and I did think our relationship had possibilities. I know this sounds silly now, but I sort of said yes. I was real hesitant. Manny was so excited he never caught my message. He went around and told everyone we were engaged until finally I had to tell him I didn't think we were ready and broke our engagement."

"Obviously, this story has a happy ending," Angela said.

"Yes, but I could have saved myself some embarrassment," said the proud expectant father. "I've learned not to push so fast. Sometimes Carol says one thing, but her tone of voice says something else. I've learned I'd better ask some questions and find out what she's really thinking."

"So you're saying there's more to listening than just words," Ted observed.

"I need to *understand*," Manny emphasized. "That means I need to notice my wife's expressions and her tone of voice. Often that means as much as her words."

"I think actions mean more than words," said Sam. "I wish I had a nickel for every time Ken said he'd pick up his room. He says, 'yeah, I'll do it' just to get me off his back. But he doesn't mean it."

Ken couldn't resist a rebuttal. "Dad, sometimes you don't take time to listen to my side. You just issue an order and that's it."

"So how can we learn to be better listeners?" Ted probed.

"I appreciate it when someone looks at me when I'm talking," offered Angela.

Robin noticed that Sue had left the table to help one of her kids. "Look at Sue over there. She's practically kneeling, looking her child in the eye. Whether she realizes it or not, she's telling her child that he's important."

"Sometimes when you talk to people, they look away like something else is on their mind," Angela continued. "That really bugs me; I'm especially thinking of someone at work. It always seems like he has something more important to think about than what

I'm saying."

"Sometimes people are too eager to say their piece before you're finished saying yours," Julie observed. "I wish they'd wait and listen to what I have to say instead of just thinking about their response."

"Ted, you're good at that!" Clark said. "That night at Sam's, you listened to what Sam said and then summarized it. You're doing the same thing today. What do you think makes a good listener?"

"Thank you for the compliment. I believe listening is a skill we *can* learn. One thing I've realized relates to what Julie just said. Sometimes our bias gets in the way. The other day in a planning session at our company, the leader of the meeting completely missed an important point because he'd already made up his mind what direction we should take. One of our men was trying diplomatically to point out some potential flaws in his plan. But at the end of the meeting, the leader said, 'Then I'll assume we're all in agreement.' We weren't in agreement but the leader's bias kept him from hearing that.

"To avoid that, one thing I try to do is ask questions first in order to try to understand what a person is thinking. Then I summarize or paraphrase what I heard back to the speaker. That doesn't mean I agree with him, but it does say I understand him."

"My boss does that well," Alice said. "After I've stated a concern, he will say, 'Let me summarize what I think I hear you saying.' After he paraphrases my statement, he asks me if he's heard me right. He answers me only after he's sure he has a clear understanding of what I've said."

"How does that make you feel?" Julie asked.

"Really good! Even if he makes a decision I don't agree with, at least I know he's considered my side."

"You don't know how fortunate you are," mumbled Sam. He was thinking about how he often exchanged statements with the director of marketing, but neither man seemed to hear what the other was saying.

Ted summarized, "So if we're going to relate well with people we need to care about them and we need to hear what they are saying — to understand them. We're really doing well. Any other ideas?"

"There's one thing Clark does that I really appreciate," Sue said. "He's always encouraging me. He does it with his clients, and he does it with me. 'You can do it,' or 'That's a great job you did.' I think that's important."

"It's sure nice to hear when you do a good job," Carol added. "My bosses tell me to do this and do that, or why didn't you do this, fix that, you missed this. I know that's important. But sometimes it's nice to hear, 'Hey, thanks for getting that contract typed so quickly. You did a good job.' "

"Or even if you wear a new dress," said Robin. "I'm kind of disappointed if I wear a new outfit to the office and no one notices."

"My mother was so good at telling me I could accomplish whatever I set my mind to do," Angela said. "When I was thinking of majoring in physics in college, she encouraged me to 'go for it.' I think that's a big reason why I was so successful."

"But there's an important point to remember," Julie interjected. "Even when you fail, it's important to know that you're still a significant person. Affirming . . . I think that's the word I want. We can affirm someone even if we disagree or there's a problem. Does that make sense?"

"It sure does," Alice nodded in agreement. "I think that's what got to me in my first marriage. The put-downs. 'How could you do such a dumb thing?' The sarcastic comments. Never anything positive like, 'I appreciate the effort you put out to make this a nice home for the family.' He didn't have to like everything I did, but he could have appreciated that I tried and that I wanted a nice home as much as he did."

"Can I give an example?" It was Ken who, aside from the one comment to his father, had sat silently through the whole discussion. "We had this guy named Stan in our PE class my junior year in high school. I mean this guy was fat and no athlete, believe me. We all made fun of him, called him 'Molasses' because he was so unbelievably slow. No one ever picked him for a team. Our PE teacher, Coach Johnson, he got tired of all our razzing and so one term he said he didn't want to hear any more put-downs. Any time we made fun of Stan or anyone else, we had to run a lap. That was the rule for the whole term. Instead, Coach said when we said anything it had to be positive. It was kind of like an experiment, see? He particularly started telling Stan that he was all right, that he could do it.

"We played a lot of basketball that quarter and any time Stan did anything remotely right, Coach praised him. Gradually some of the rest of us started doing the same thing. It was hard at first. What do you say when someone completely misses a pass that's right on his hands? Or shoots the ball clear over the backboard? Maybe it was just, 'Hey, you tried. Next time you'll do better.'

"Well, the last week we had a basketball tournament, and Stan was on my team. Now we had a couple of good players and we wanted to win the tournament, but how do you win with Stan on your team? Well, we decided we were going to try and we told Stan he'd improved a lot and we believed in him and we were going to win this thing. And wouldn't you know it, we got to the championship

game. Stan hadn't scored a point in the tournament, but he worked
hard and got some rebounds. Well, the final game is tied and time's
running out and all of a sudden there's five seconds left and Stan
has the ball. He can't find anyone to throw it to and we yell, 'Shoot.'
And so he shoots the ball and wouldn't you know it, it goes in!

"You should have seen us. We went crazy pounding Stan on
the back and saying, 'Way to go, Molasses!' It was really an incredible
experience."

"That just shows how powerful encouragement and affirmation
are," Ted said. "Thanks for telling us that story. This has been great.
I suppose we ought to get back to work and finish putting up this
playground equipment. Sam, what do you think? Has this been
helpful?"

"I think so." Some of the points had been uncomfortable, but
he saw the overall value of what was said. "As far as the one guy
at work, I think I can listen to him a little more. My tendency is
to cut him off when he starts harping about production. Maybe I
should listen a little more, another couple of minutes, and try to
understand his perspective."

"This discussion's helped me, too," Alice said. "Teri — she's
my junior high daughter — and I have had our differences lately.
She'll come in and want to talk right when I'm in the middle of
fixing dinner or something. You've got to understand, I don't have
a lot of time to work and run a household and get everything done.
But maybe it wouldn't hurt for me to relax for a moment and listen
to her. She has a short attention span so it probably wouldn't mean
but another five minutes. That's just saying to her that I care, and
she's worth listening to, and she's important."

"Which perfectly sums up what we've been saying!" Ted concluded.

The group rose and resumed their work on the playground
project. Several women started clearing the table and covering the
food. As they did, Alice said, "By the way, ladies, you'll be getting
an invitation in a few days. I'm having a little party to sell some
nice stationery. There will be a special sale on Christmas cards.
However, you don't have to buy anything. Since this is my first show,
it would mean a lot if you could just come."

"Sounds like a good opportunity to apply what we just learned!"
Sue said.

"I'll be there," said Julie and a couple of the other women.

That night, Ted spent a few minutes jotting down the highlights
of the discussion. "See what you think of this, Amy. Here's three
ways to help achieve your potential and enjoy life more through
better relationships with people."

ENJOY "QUALITY" RELATIONSHIPS

● **C** ARE—Let people know they are important
● **H** EAR—Listen until you understand
● **A** FFIRM—Let people know they are doing well

"I like that," Amy responded. "I'd never really thought about how relationships affect our potential. But we really can't succeed independent of others. And you know, if we're caring, listening, and affirming to others, they're more likely to be the same back to us."

"I agree. That's simply treating others the way we like to be treated." He looked at his notes for a moment and observed, "Something's missing here. We don't have anything about communicating our thoughts to others. I think we'll come back and develop this some more later."

"Alice invited the ladies to a stationery party next week. Maybe we'll have a chance to talk some more then. You know, I'm intrigued by what Alice is accomplishing. I'd like to find out how she gets so much done."

"Then why don't you be my ears and eyes at that meeting! I'd like to find out what you learn."

*One of the secrets to personal
growth: exploring new areas of
knowledge and skill and selecting those that are right for you.*

5

EXPANDED HORIZONS

Alice's party was a tremendous success. No one could
believe that this was her first formal presentation of Cards and Paper
Supreme. All the ladies agreed it was a thoroughly professional
program and display. The dining room table had a colorful array of
note paper, greeting cards, wrapping paper, calendars, and stickers.
Featured were Christmas items, with a chance to shop at great prices.
Nearly everyone bought something, and two women signed up to
host parties.

Several guests had left but most of the neighborhood women
continued to visit in Alice's living room. Ginny Harris had even come
and ordered some Christmas cards before politely excusing herself
after refreshments were served. Earlier in the week, Angela had made
it a point to invite Ginny to the party. "I don't think her husband is
feeling well," Angela said after Ginny left. "Plus, he's under a lot
of pressure at work, and Ginny's really concerned."

"She was very quiet," Julie said. "Do you think she had a good
time?"

"She really wanted to come. But she doesn't like to be away

from Bob for very long."

"I'm sure glad I could come," said Julie. "Sam wasn't excited about putting the kids to bed, but he did it. I think our neighborhood brainstorming session helped. One night last week, we sat down after dinner and had a long talk."

"That's great!" Sue responded.

"Well, it is an improvement. I still can't get him to tell me what's really on his mind. But he did listen to me and I think he tried to understand my feelings about a couple of things."

"That's a start," Amy agreed. "You can't expect him to change overnight."

"Alice, this was a fun meeting!" Sue said. The other women agreed. "You were so professional," said one. "It's obvious you put a lot of work into it," said another.

"Thanks. I really appreciate your encouragement. It means a lot that you'd come out and support me like this."

Carol wanted to know how Alice managed so well. "I don't think I could do all you do — full-time job, three kids, a second job — and your house is so beautiful."

"Thanks. I guess I've learned that you don't know what you can do until you try. After my divorce, I decided to expand my borders and learn some new skills. I figured I could feel sorry for myself, or I could get busy and find something I enjoyed doing that could provide some more income for our family. So here I am, selling stationery."

"Clark's the salesman in our family," Sue laughed. "You've got a great product, but I don't think I could sell anything."

"I didn't think so either. But I had to do something. With the divorce settlement, I was able to buy this house and, supposedly, have some monthly child support . . . but that's very irregular. My job at the bank covers the necessities. But I want to do more for my kids without having to be away from home any more than necessary. So I evaluated my options. I didn't feel comfortable doing any crafts. I didn't like the idea of phone sales. Going to night school was an option, but it meant being away from the kids too much. So I thought maybe I ought to at least examine selling something out of my home."

"You must have gotten some training to do this?" Sue asked.

"Yes, that's one of the things that attracted me. This company provides excellent training. I found I didn't have to go back to school to learn what I needed. They provided books, tapes, and seminars."

"I'm curious, Alice, how did you choose this particular product?" Amy asked. "Bringing a stationery store to our homes is really a great idea."

"Well, first I decided to examine some options. I must have attended a dozen different parties for various products this year. You know — detergents, vitamins, weight loss programs, jewelry, crystal, cosmetics, and so on. I asked a lot of questions, not just about the product, but what the company does to support its sales people. I wanted to sell a product I really used and believed in, but I also wanted a company that would invest some time in me so that I was equipped to do a professional job. Cards and Paper Supreme had a great concept, plus plenty of support to the seller. For example, they provide training tapes that I can listen to during the forty minutes I spend driving to and from work. They also have the most thorough manual I've seen. Many nights after the kids are in bed, I spend time studying it. There are many other things I could have done, but this seems right for me."

"I tried selling a cosmetics line for a while," Julie said. "I guess it was five or six years ago. I didn't enjoy it. So now when someone tries to get me involved in another venture like that, it's easy to turn it down. I don't regret trying it, but I learned that I'd much rather involve myself in some community projects."

"Ted had the opposite experience," said Amy. "He never intended to sell insurance, but one summer while he was in college, he decided to try something different. He took a door-to-door sales job selling encyclopedias."

"Now that's a challenge," Sue said. "Clark says he'd never do that. He doesn't like having doors slammed in his face."

"Ted found it a challenge to find ways to keep the doors open. He says he learned a lot of important people skills, and after he graduated, he decided to become an insurance agent. I don't think he would have taken that kind of job if he hadn't first sold encyclopedias for a summer."

Angela observed how she felt it was important for her to try new things, and it was also fun. "Some people never stretch themselves. They get a job, work nine to five, then come home and watch TV and that's it. They don't come close to fulfilling their potential. Say, that relates to our project, doesn't it? This is an important part of achieving our potential. We need to try different things, if for no other reason than to expand our range of experiences. When I was in college, I switched majors a couple of times. But after I decided to major in physics, I still took some extra courses just because I was curious about them. For example, I took classes in anthropology, modern dance, and medieval literature. They weren't required; I just wanted to take them. I'm still doing things like that. Last year I learned how to make stained glass windows. It was something I'd always wanted to do, so I did it."

Amy felt that her past experience helped her make decisions now. "Recently I was asked to lead a youth choir. I know how to do that, but I've never really enjoyed it — I prefer playing or teaching piano. So I declined."

"You know what I find in all this?" asked Angela, full of enthusiasm. "You really can't lose. No matter what happens, when you try something new, you learn. Even if you learn it's not your area of skill or interest, that's valuable information. For example, I think my roommate has learned a lot living in this neighborhood, right Robin?"

Robin blushed at being put on the spot. "I've always lived in an apartment and I tend to be rather shy about reaching out and meeting people. This has been a good experience for me, especially being around your families."

"And Robin signed up for a computer course. Why don't you tell us about that?"

"My boss asked me to take the course. He said he thought I could do well. I wasn't so sure, but it's going OK."

"You won't regret it," said Carol. "I know I was uncomfortable the first time I started on the computer at our law firm. But I get so much more done now. The only problem is that there's so much more I could do with our system, but I haven't learned it yet."

"Have you thought about taking some time occasionally just to experiment with your computer?" asked Amy.

"What do you mean?"

"When you have a little slack time — or occasionally you could take a few minutes during a break — try something new. You might open the manual once a week and try a new function. That way you could get better acquainted with the software. My husband is often experimenting. This is kind of a crazy example, but he does some incredible things with paper clips and rubber bands. I've told him he ought to write a book about it. Once he was in a hotel in Europe and he'd forgotten to bring a special plug for something. He rigged up one with a couple of paper clips and rubber bands, and it worked. I'm glad I wasn't with him; I didn't think that was a very safe thing to do."

"It's amazing what you can do when you have to," Angela said. "We wouldn't have synthetic rubber if it hadn't been for World War II when we were cut off from our rubber supply."

"I see what you mean," Carol said. "But I'd feel a little more confident if there were someone to coach me."

"Then why not ask an expert?" Angela suggested. "I carry a little tape recorder with me for my job and when I need some information, I find an expert and see if I can ask a few questions.

Then I turn on the recorder so I don't have to worry about taking notes right then. I find most people like talking about their area of expertise, and I think that's especially true of computer buffs."

"I don't know why I haven't thought of that," Robin said. "I ought to record my computer class so I can review it later. Then I don't have to worry about taking so many notes. My instructor is a good teacher, but it still gets confusing."

"That's a good idea, but don't be afraid to ask questions, either," Angela said. "For a while I wouldn't ask questions I thought others might consider dumb. I don't do that any more, because I feel it's more important to know the answer. I've never had anyone say, 'That's a dumb question.' Maybe they think it sometimes, but at least I learn what I need to know."

Amy made an observation. "I think we're saying that it's very important to look around and check our options. But sooner or later, we need to buy into something. Carol and Robin, you can explore or try the many functions of your computers, but then you need to decide which ones you're really going to use. Alice, you looked around for a few months but you finally decided to go with this one company and focus on learning its product."

Alice agreed. "That's a good point. I could have kept on looking for the perfect situation, and frankly, I never would have found it. There are so many products and opportunities, I could never examine them all. Maybe that's why I set an arbitrary limit on the time I would spend looking for a second income. I made a checklist of things I wanted to have — like flexible hours, working out of my home, a product I believed in, solid training and support, good income potential, and so on. Many of the things I saw had some of those elements. None had all. But this one came closest to meeting all of my objectives."

"Sounds like it helped, though, when you wrote that down," Sue observed.

"That's true. In fact, let me show you the notebook I kept." Alice went to a desk by her kitchen phone and pulled out a small three-ring notebook. "Here on the first page I wrote out my objectives. Then I kept a little journal of each product party I attended, a summary of my observations, how it matched against my objectives, and so on. This way I didn't forget what I was learning."

"Ted does that same kind of thing with his 3 x 5 cards," said Amy. "He's always writing ideas down. He also keeps a little notepad with him all the time for illustrations. He has to make a lot of speeches for his company and so any time he hears a good joke or story, he jots it down. He must have a thousand illustrations by now."

"He'll never be able to use all those."

"That's true — but when he hears a story, he doesn't evaluate whether he'll use it or not. He writes it down so when the time comes to prepare a speech, he has it available among his options. And this is another point. Ted says that while he's always learning, he needs those deadlines when he's got to make a speech or write an article because it forces him to make decisions on what he believes and what stories are most effective to illustrate his points."

"My tape recorder helps me in the same way," Angela said. "When we have a brainstorming session in our department, I like to get all our ideas on a project. Not everything said is pertinent, but it helps me understand what everyone's thinking. Later, I sift through the material and decide what's most important."

"I keep a diary," Carol offered, tentatively.

"That's a good thing to do," Amy said. "What do you put in it?"

"Well, I note anything special we've done that day. And sometimes I write down my thoughts or ideas."

"Do you ever go back and look over it?"

"Well, not very often."

"The reason I ask is because I keep a journal and periodically I go back and review what I've learned. I find it helps put things in perspective. For example, suppose I'm struggling with one of my teenagers. Just reviewing some past situations I've recorded on paper gives me hope that I will survive this crisis, too. And sometimes I get ideas from what worked or didn't work in the past, so I'm building on what I've learned."

"Alice," Sue asked, "I'm curious; how did you actually make your decision? I see how you gathered all the information, but it seems that, unless the choice was really obvious, it could get kind of confusing. How did you *know* this was right for you?"

"Let me show you," Alice said. She turned a few pages in her notebook and then showed the women the following:

2ND JOB DECISION

ALTERNATIVES

OBJECTIVES	Sharp Cutlery	Cards & Paper	Magic Makeup
Product I Use	–	+	+
Training	0	+	–
Financial Potential	–	+	0
TOTAL	-2	+3	0

"This is what I call a decision chart," Alice explained. "Across the top I listed my top three alternatives. All of these companies have quality products and I wouldn't mind selling any of them. But I had to choose one. Down the left side, I listed my three primary criteria. First, I wanted to sell a product I used. That is a personal conviction — that I need to believe enough in the product to use it in my home. Second, as I've already stated, I wanted a solid training program for company reps. And third, I wanted maximum income potential for the time I invested. So I was looking for a product most people would probably use, and where there was a significant chance people would reorder regularly.

"The chart is completed by putting a plus, minus or zero according to whether the alternative accomplishes, doesn't accomplish or is ____ l relative to an objective. So for Sharp Cutlery, I have ____ and minus for the three options. The reason I don't use ____ is because I already own an excellent set of knives. ____ re's no question I'd buy their line; it's probably the best ____ Cards and Paper I put all pluses. As I've already said, ____ r Supreme had the most complete training package. ____ Makeup I put a plus, minus and zero, but I felt it would be difficult to motivate women to change their brand of makeup. So you can see how I rated each alternative according to my objectives. Someone else with a different set of objectives might come up with a different conclusion. When I completed the chart, I totalled each column and, in this case, it was obvious what was best for me."

Angela commented, "That's an excellent process. But what would happen if you wound up with a tie?"

"Then I would more carefully evaluate if one of my objectives was more important and double its value. For example, I might have felt that the training was twice as important as the other two objectives. So I'd put two pluses, or two minuses and retotal the columns."

"Wow! Your chart really makes sense," Carol said. "It's so clear, and when you've made your decision, you have reasons to be confident that it's the right decision."

"I could see how this could be used when buying a car or deciding which neighborhood to live in," Julie added. "I just thought of an example that illustrates all we've been saying. It's a lot like shopping. Alice, you went shopping for a second job. When I purchase an applicance for my house, I visit several stores. It's different from window shopping. We all do that sometimes — just go around the mall and look with no intention of buying anything. But I'm talking about viewing something to see if it fits my need. If I'm buying a refrigerator, for example, I mentally picture how it would look in my kitchen. If I'm shopping for a dress, I actually try on a number of dresses. Then I need to make a choice. So the second step is to buy the item that's right for me. I can't use the refrigerator or dress until I buy it. So Alice, you checked out a number of options to see what might fit your situation. When you decided what was right for you, you bought into it."

"And tonight, some of you were window shoppers, and some of you were buyers!" said Alice with a laugh, and the rest of the group laughed with her.

"You did say we could just come and look!"

"And I meant it. But taking Julie's example even further, we can try something; we can even buy it; but if we don't use it, it doesn't do us any good. To put it another way, I could get all the training about how to sell Cards and Paper Supreme products, I could order catalogs and inventory, but sooner or later I had to invite people to a party and actually attempt to sell."

"You have to use it or apply it," Amy emphasized. "My husband once spent a lot of time shopping for a camera. He finally bought a really nice one, used it for a couple of weeks, and that was it. It just sits around and I end up taking most of our family pictures with my old Instamatic. He isn't 'using' it."

"I want to ask Alice something," Carol said. "I still don't see how you find the time to do this with all of your other responsibilities."

"To be honest, it's not easy. That's where I needed to do some planning. I've checked various alternatives. I feel I've made a good decision to sell this stationery. Now I need to follow through. I did that by asking three basic questions. First, *what* do I want to accomplish? Well, to be specific, I decided I wanted to hold two parties a month to present and sell Cards and Paper Supreme products. Next, I asked *how* I am going to do that. For me, that meant studying the manual, making a checklist of things to do, ordering my displays, and so on. Also, it meant counting the cost. For instance, there was the initial investment of capital to start the business. Also, there were some questions I needed answered; I needed to find out what resources were available to answer those questions. Then third, I asked *when* I was going to do this. I wrote down on my calendar when to study, when to order supplies, when to hold my first party, when to send out invitations, and so on. I've already scheduled an evening to make some phone calls to schedule more parties. My point is, it doesn't just happen. I must systematically plan to follow through.

"Frankly, in order to do that, I had to adjust my schedule. I had to evaluate how I was spending my time each day and see if there was anything I could do without. Well, at night after the kids were in bed I had a couple of hours to myself. Often I used that time just to relax and watch TV. I decided that I could use some of that time to better advantage. I still watch a good movie on TV, but I don't let myself watch a whole series of shows one after the other."

Amy saw what Alice was saying. "It's easy for us to just wish something would happen. Alice, you tell us you finally bought into Cards and Paper Supreme. Then you developed a system to work it into your schedule."

Angela had another example that illustrated each of the points made so far. "A couple of years ago I was frustrated because I wasn't staying in good physical condition. I decided I wanted to get back into good shape and I evaluated a number of options — jogging, swimming, joining a health club, jumping rope, so on. I could realistically do any one of those, but when it came to selecting one that worked best for me, I chose jumping rope. So how did I apply it? I bought a rope and decided to jump rope for ten minutes every morning before I showered and headed for work. It's become a part of my daily routine."

"So what we're saying is that we try things," said Amy. "Then we buy into one — we decide to do something. Finally we apply — that's the planning and follow-through process that allows us to work the details into our busy lives."

"That's right," Alice said. "I think what I've realized is that there are a lot of exciting opportunities in life. After my divorce, I could have sat around and had a pity party. Or I could do something. I've decided I want to achieve my potential. Sure, I've had a bad experience, but my life isn't over. There's a lot I can do. I had to try some things to find out what was right for me. Now I have something and I'm moving forward."

Sue gave a loud sigh and everyone turned to her. "All of this is so good. But it's also discouraging. Alice, at least your kids are older. You've got some control of your time. I've got two preschoolers. They're always demanding my attention. Sometimes it seems like I never have any time of my own. When I do start something, I can count on an interruption. And then Clark gets home and I need to fix dinner and spend time with him . . ."

Several of the women nodded with understanding. They'd been there. Carol didn't have children, but she commented, "I think my job is preparing me for kids. I have three bosses, and I'm always getting interrupted to do a higher priority project. That's the story of my life."

Angela rose and asked to be excused. "I'd love to keep talking, but I have to go to work tomorrow."

"So do I," Carol said. "Maybe we can talk about this topic another time."

It was late and so the party broke up. Amy thanked Alice for the evening. "I'm going to give Ted a report. I know he will want to add the contents of our discussion to his notebook." Then she put an arm around Sue and said, "I think I know what you're feeling. I can assure you this won't last forever. But there is one important lesson I learned when my children were young that actually helped me to appreciate their interruptions. If you're interested, maybe we can talk about it sometime soon."

"Oh yes! I can use any help you can give me."

Amy and Carol walked home together. Along the way, Amy invited Carol and her husband to come over for dinner the following weekend. "It will give us a chance to get better acquainted, and maybe we can talk about how to handle those interruptions." Carol quickly accepted.

Ted was very interested in Amy's report. He had her review the highlights of the conversation and then asked, "Do you think you can summarize the essence of the discussion in a handful of points?"

"Yes, I think so. First, we talked about how, if we are going to achieve our potential, we need to look around and try different things." As Ted listened, he jotted some notes in his notebook.

"Second, we also need to make decisions and buy into the things that are right for us. If necessary, we may make a chart so the decision is clear. We also mentioned how time limits can force us to make decisions so we're not always looking and never accomplishing anything. Then third, we said we had to plan to apply the things we said we were going to do. I told them about how you shopped for a camera and then bought it, but you never use it now."

"I use it once in a while!" Ted protested good-naturedly.

"Maybe once a year, at Christmas! But the point is, if we buy something and then let it sit idle, it's useless. A lot of people never fulfill their potential, even though they have great opportunities, because they don't apply what they have."

"Can you tell me a little more about the chart?"

"Alice listed her options across the top of the chart. Then down the left side, she wrote down her objectives or criteria for making her decision. Then under each option she put a plus sign for each objective that was met, and minus sign for those that weren't, and a zero if it was in-between. Then she totalled each column."

"So she knew what option was best for her," Ted concluded. "We use decision charts at work on occasion, but Alice's is simpler. I really like it." Ted was also enthusiastic about his wife's report. "Amy, that's really easy to remember! Try, Buy, Apply. TBA." He showed her his notes:

GROW TOWARD YOUR POTENTIAL

- **T** RY—Be open to grow and learn new skills
- **B** UY—Make a good decision on what to apply
- **A** PPLY—Plan to implement your decisions

"That's it!" Amy laughed. "You know, I think this builds on

what we discussed with Clark and Sue a few weeks ago. We talked about discovering our strengths. But we can also grow in our areas of weakness. In fact, we're really not limited because we can develop in some areas that may have been weaknesses and build them until they are actually strengths."

"Which is what Alice is doing," Ted observed. "She had a need and she looked around and experimented until she found what was right for her. Now she's building new strengths and skills and she's enjoying life more as a result."

As they concluded their discussion, Amy mentioned her discussion with Sue and Carol about handling interruptions. "I'd like to invite both of them over soon. I think they'd be interested in learning how to roll with the benefits."

*How to achieve your potential
and enjoy life even when you
are interrupted "all the time."*

6

ROLL WITH
THE BENEFITS

T he Simpsons and Riesses enjoyed a relaxed dinner. Carol told how she'd heard the baby's heartbeat for the first time during her most recent visit to the obstetrician. Fortunately, her bouts with morning sickness were over now and her only complaint was that she was beginning to look big. She had always prided herself on her appearance.

Amy tried out the *"TRY, BUY, APPLY"* outline on Manny and Carol over dessert. Manny liked it. "When you're aggressively trying new things, that opens up all sorts of possibilities, doesn't it?"

"Are you thinking of your photography?" Carol asked.

"Yes. My dream is someday to make a living as a photographer. But I'd have to specialize — do primarily portraits, or nature photography, or weddings, or run a processing lab. Amy, your outline gives me an idea. I could study several kinds of photography and try them out. I could enter different contests, try selling my photos to magazines, shoot some weddings, shoot some portraits, do some creative/artsy stuff. That would be the *Try* part."

"Good thinking. What about *Buy?*" asked Ted.

"After some time, I'm thinking maybe five years, I'd need to zero in on one or two areas where I really want to focus and become more proficient. Then I'd begin to set up a business that I could operate as a second job."

"So now you're into *Apply.*"

"Right! I'd set up a studio, or whatever, and I'd really concentrate on making it a successful business. It might take a few more years, but eventually I would hope I could do it full-time."

"That sounds good, Manny," said Ted. "Now you're taking your dream — your objective — and developing a plan to help you get there."

As Amy poured coffee for her guests, she mentioned that she'd invited Sue to join them. "Carol, remember when Sue expressed her frustration with interruptions, and you expressed similar frustration concerning your work? Ted and I thought we might talk about that this evening."

Sue arrived a few minutes later. "Clark said he'd look after the kids. But he's so engrossed in a ball game . . . I hope nothing happens. My two kids could destroy half the house and Clark wouldn't know it."

"Amy says she wants to discuss the issue you raised last week," Carol said. "How bad is it with kids, really? I want to achieve my potential, but with the baby coming and all, I'm just wondering . . ."

"It really wasn't all that bad with the first child," Sue explained. "But when the second one came, that was a different story. With just Leslie, I usually had a block of time each day when she was taking a nap and I could get things done. But with two, it seems that, at least so far, there's always something to interrupt me."

"I remember those days," Amy reflected. "You're right. For several years, it seemed like I could rarely plan my own schedule. I tend to be a disciplined person. Even before I was married I set goals and managed my time fairly well. After the kids were born and I stopped teaching, I decided to discipline myself to practice piano at least an hour a day. But I probably missed my time as often as I made it, and that frustrated me to no end. Often just as I sat down and started practicing one of the kids would come and say he needed a diaper changed or big brother hit him or he wanted something to eat or, sometimes, he just wanted my attention."

"That's my situation exactly," Sue said. "One of the things I like to do is study decorating magazines. Often I'll sit down and my two-year-old will come over and knock the magazine out of my hand. That's his way of saying he wants my attention."

"You probably resent that interruption, don't you?"

"Well, yes. Especially if I've been with him all day. Sometimes

I'll tell him I need a few minutes alone and he'll go play by himself. But then the kids will start fighting, or one of them will get hurt, or for whatever reason I'll have to stop what I'm doing and go take care of some emergency."

"The frustration is real," Amy recalled from her own experience. "It's tempting just to say 'I won't schedule my time, because I can't follow my plans anyway.' But I don't think that's the solution. And let me add that, the problem isn't just at home. Some people are frustrated at work because they're frequently interrupted by things like the phone."

"In my work, I've tried to be diligent and schedule major projects I need to do each day," said Carol. "But I'd say it's a rare day when I complete all those projects. Inevitably something 'more important' is inserted into the schedule."

"So do you stop scheduling those jobs?" Amy asked.

"Well, no. That helps me know what's priority. So when no one is pushing something in front of me, I always know how to make the best use of my time. I'm always doing something important."

"That's exactly the point!" Amy said, with such enthusiasm that the ladies were surprised. "I did the same thing! I decided to continue setting goals and planning and even scheduling. You see, even with the children around, there were periods of time every day where I had some control, even if it wasn't total control. What I did was write down all the types of time periods for a typical day. There were times when all the kids were awake and at home. Times when they were in school, or taking naps. Times when one was awake and another napping — and so on. For each time period, I thought of activities I could do. When the kids were napping or in school, I could do a major project; maybe clean the house, or practice piano. With one child around, playing by himself, I could do other kinds of activities where it wasn't a problem if I was interrupted. With all of this in my mind, I realized I could always make good use of my time.

"So let me think back a few years. Suppose one of my kids was in school and the other two were taking their afternoon naps. Usually they slept a couple of hours, but this time one of them only slept twenty minutes. So I didn't get the block of time I'd anticipated. At first I was frustrated because my schedule was ruined. But then I learned to shift. Instead of thinking about what I couldn't do, I thought of the benefits of the new situation — what I could do."

"The benefits of the interruption?" Sue asked.

"Yes. In fact, after a while I stopped thinking of it as an interruption. I couldn't change the situation; the child was awake. So instead I viewed it as an opportunity to spend quality time with the one child. Time with that child became number one priority instead of my project. Or if he wanted to play by himself, I'd fold laundry or unload the dishwasher or make a phone call . . . some activity I needed to get done that day, but where it didn't matter if I was interrupted again. I called it 'rolling with the benefits.'

"As the kids got older, my time became more predictable. But even today, the kids can still change my plans. I try to remember that when one of them comes to me with a need; meeting that need becomes my top priority."

"When I saw Amy doing this, I learned an important concept," Ted said. "I used to get frustrated at work with certain phone interruptions. Especially from a couple of small clients who took up far more time than I thought they warranted. I decided that when I got a phone call I didn't want, I would make myself think of two benefits of that interruption.

"Suppose, for example, Jack calls. He's a nitpicker for detail and I don't like taking time to answer all of his little questions. But I sold his company a policy and I need to service him. Instead of thinking, *What a waste of time,* I'd think, *Jack is a thorough person; I can learn from him. And he has influence in his company. Someday my relationship with Jack could lead to a major group policy from his firm.* By the time I've thought of two benefits of this interruption, I'm into the conversation and my whole attitude about talking with Jack has changed."

"That sounds like an easier way to go through life," Manny observed.

"Exactly! You're saving energy for more productive uses. So many people waste valuable emotional energy thinking about all the things wrong with their situation."

"So you're saying I should look at my interruptions as good for me?" asked Carol. "I'm not sure I follow."

"Let's talk about your job, Carol. Do you do all the typing in the office?"

"No. We have a receptionist and another typist, plus we send some of our work out to a typing service. Some of our dictation is routine — letters, memos. Some of the documents are also routine; we just have to change the names, dates, that sort of thing. I'm in charge of appointment schedules, and they give me the special projects. They say I'm the most accurate typist and they have to spend less time giving me instructions."

"Sounds like you're a very valuable employee."

Carol beamed at Ted's compliment.

"These lawyers obviously trust you," Ted said. "When they give you a job, time is of the essence. They're saying, 'This is important.' Getting an urgent document out might mean thousands of dollars to a client. Or make the crucial difference in an upcoming trial. They're saying, 'We can't afford to mess up, so we'll give it to Carol.' Isn't that right?"

"Yes, I suppose so."

"If it weren't that important, any other typist could do it. So when they interrupt you with a rush job, does that mean they don't like you? No, it means they are very glad you're their employee. They need you! That's why they're paying you good money."

"I hadn't thought of it in quite that way."

"Suppose you get interrupted by the telephone. An important client needs to talk to one of the lawyers but he's tied up. If he's interrupted, that hinders his effectiveness. His client can't afford for him to be inefficient. So you take the call, and you schedule the appointment. That's your job. That's what makes you so very valuable. That's the benefit of having you there."

"Sue, the same concept is true at home," Amy said. "How would you feel if your children had a need and no one was there to help?"

"I'd feel terrible. That's one reason I decided not to go back to work until the kids are in school."

"Have you ever thought of the long-term benefits of having this time with them now?"

"I think they're more secure. I know they're getting the best care I can give them. They're eating right. Not watching the wrong kind of TV shows. They're hearing good stories and learning the things I feel they need to learn."

"So by dealing with those interruptions now, you and your children will benefit for many years, maybe an entire lifetime. So you really aren't giving up your personal goals; you are just realizing that there are many elements to your plan. Right now a very important element involves your children. For a while, they must be your priority. But it won't be long before they won't require as much of your attention, and then you can make some further progress toward your other goals."

Ted wanted to remind Sue of another concept they had discussed with Clark a few weeks earlier. "Carol, this might help you, too. Clark and I talked with Sam about having a standard work day and arranging that standard day according to how we can be most productive. Well, another element of that is to recognize our natural tendencies. We all have a natural energy cycle, and we should recognize that and make the most of it."

"I'm a morning person," Amy said, who saw where her husband was taking the conversation. "I'm up and raring to go at 6:00 in the morning. But after 9:00 at night, I'm a basket case. Don't expect me to make any important decisions at night. Now Ted, he starts slow, but often his most creative times are late at night."

"There's a guy in my office who works standing up," said Ted. "When I first met him, I asked him why he worked at a stand-up desk. His answer made sense: 'I've never fallen asleep standing up.' He explained that often after lunch he felt drowsy and when he'd come back to his office and sit in his overstuffed chair, he wasn't very productive. He found that when he stood up and walked around, he got a lot more done. That's a man who recognizes his natural tendencies and takes advantage of them."

"My kids are night owls," Sue complained. "Clark and I have tried to put them to bed by 8:00 so we can have some time alone. But it's such a hassle. They just won't go to sleep."

"Are you a morning person?" Ted asked.

"Yes. Sometimes I feel like I get more done in the first two hours than I do the rest of the day."

"Have you ever considered letting your kids stay up later so they'll sleep later in the morning and give you some more time to yourself?"

"No. But now that I think about it, that might be worth a try."

"Maybe you and Clark could have breakfast together before the kids are up," Amy suggested.

"He is a big breakfast eater. I'll talk to him about it. Maybe we ought to just spend that additional evening time with the kids."

"That's going with your and the family's natural tendencies," Amy said. "If your kids won't go to sleep, you're obviously fighting a frustrating battle trying to make them go to bed early. So maybe you can relax and adjust your schedule. You'll get more done and you'll enjoy the family more."

Ted and Amy were so engrossed in the discussion that they didn't notice Manny taking a few candid photos, using only the available light in the room. In the moment of silence following Amy's last comment, everyone heard the click of Manny's camera catching Ted as he gently squeezed his wife's hand. When Amy looked over at Manny in surprise, he gave her a big smile. "Gotcha!"

Manny put his camera down and mentioned that he had never realized how good he had it until this discussion. "Of course, we don't have any kids right now," he laughed. "But I also don't have any interruptions on my job. I drive a truck, so I actually have a lot of time to think about other things."

"As long as you pay attention to the highway," Carol said.

"Sure, I have to do my job, but what I'm saying is that it doesn't occupy all my thoughts."

"Is there anything in particular you do with that time?"

"I try to use my time twice. I always take my camera with me, and when I take a rest stop, I often shoot pictures. In the cab, I have a tape deck — so sometimes I listen to tapes of seminars on photography. And I always take a photography magazine or book along with me. When I stop for a bite to eat, I usually read. So while I'm driving a truck, I'm also learning more about photography."

"I think that's a very important concept," Ted added. "There are a lot of ways we can use our time twice."

"But how do you do that if you don't drive a truck?" Sue asked.

"Ted and I often spend time together talking while we do the dishes or clean a room," said Amy. "And Ted almost never runs an errand without taking one of the kids along. The kids love that special time with Dad."

"In fact, that's doing three things at once!" said Ted. "It gives Amy a break. It gives me time with one of my kids. And I have to do the errand anyway."

"Plus, Ted usually piggy-backs his errands so he gets as many done as possible. He hates running just one errand. He saves them up so he can do as many as possible in one trip. And then he plans the route. I've seen him make out a list of what he needs to do in town, and he'll number them so he takes the most efficient path."

"That's true. I find a minute or two spent planning my trip can save an hour or more traveling back and forth across town."

"I wish Clark could hear this," Sue lamented. "He's admitted he doesn't make the best use of his time."

Ted nodded in agreement. "That's easy to let happen when you're on the road a lot like he is. One thing I've learned to do is take work with me. So if I get to an appointment and have to wait ten minutes, I have something in my brief case that I can do with that time. I call them my 'nook and cranny' jobs. There are lots of little nooks and crannies in our days, ten minutes here, five minutes there. If I'm prepared, I can take advantage of those times."

"But that doesn't do much to help you with the big projects," Carol said.

"Not necessarily. But it often helps a great deal. I have a project right now, a magazine article I need to write about a management system used by our company. I'll have to schedule a block of time a couple of weeks from now to sit down and write it. But until then, I use the 'swiss cheese' method. I take a little nibble here, a little nibble there, and put some holes in it. For example, say I'm driving to work in the morning and there's an accident on the highway. Traffic is delayed ten minutes. There's a little time where I can give some thought to the article. I might jot down some ideas on a 3 x 5 card, or dictate them into my tape recorder. Yesterday, I thought through a possible outline for the article. I've got a file of ideas, examples, and points I need to make. When I finally sit down to write the article, a lot of the work will be done."

"Ted's thought of a lot of ways to multiply his time," Amy said. "But maybe equally important is that he rarely just sits around. Take his television watching habits, for example. Once or twice a week he watches the news. And occasionally the family watches a special."

"Did you know that the average person watches nearly four hours of television every day?" Ted asked. "That's more than 1,400 hours a year! Now let me say that I don't think all television is a waste of time. But I think you'll agree that there are a lot of other ways to use 1,400 hours. If I take half that time — 700 hours — and devote it to some projects that help me achieve one of my objectives, then I'm moving that much closer to achieving my potential."

"This has really been encouraging," Sue said, as she began to gather her things. "I need to get home and relieve Clark."

"Have you gotten any helpful ideas?"

"Oh, yes. I think I'm going to try putting the kids down later at night and see if I can take better advantage of my time in the morning. And I like the idea of thinking through the benefits of my interruptions. That should allow me to relax and enjoy my family more."

As Sue was escorted to the door, Amy mentioned that she was thinking of having a neighborhood caroling party shortly before Christmas. "I thought we'd sing on some of the neighboring streets, then have some refreshments."

"Could we have the refreshments at our house?" Carol volunteered. The three women agreed on the idea and Amy said she'd find a date and coordinate it with the rest of the neighbors.

After the guests had left and the dishes and kitchen were cleaned, Ted thought about the evening's discussion. In his notebook, he wrote:

ROLL WITH THE BENEFITS

● **R** ECOGNIZE the positive side of
      interruptions (the benefits)
● **E** MPLOY your natural tendencies
● **D** OUBLE up on your time

He looked at the first letters of the last three lines. *RED*. He sat back and thought about how some people got angry and saw red when they were interrupted. But rolling with the benefits was different. In this context, Ted saw the color red as bright and positive.

This project was going better than Ted had imagined. Almost all of the neighbors were enthusiastic participants and contributors. But where would all of this lead? Would they actually find ways to apply these principles to their lives long enough to make them new habits — good habits that allowed them to achieve their potential? Well, there was a Christmas party coming up soon. That would be a good time, five months since he'd issued the challenge, to see how his neighborhood friends were doing.

*Beyond good intentions to
persistence, accountability and
discipline.*

7

INCREASING
THE FOLLOW-THROUGH

The spirit of Christmas and the warmth of friendship cancelled out the chilling effects of a cold December night. Six of the seven households on Fir Court had become a choir. They paraded down Jackson Avenue and sang Christmas carols on several of the neighboring streets. Now as they moved toward Manny and Carol's home for hot cider and dessert, someone suggested they first sing to Bob and Ginny, the only couple who had not joined in the festive celebration.

The older couple stood at the door as their neighbors sang a rousing rendition of "Joy to the World," a tender "O Little Town of Bethlehem," and finally, "We Wish You a Merry Christmas." Bob and Ginny seemed appreciative and Angela went up and gave Ginny a gentle hug. "We'd love to have you join us at Manny and Carol's," she said.

"Thanks so much," Ginny answered. "But we're really not dressed for that. Maybe next time."

Several of the women had baked Christmas cookies which they laid out on the dining room table as Carol and Sue heated the cider and made coffee. Manny was the first to sample the pastries. "Don't eat too many, hon," Carol said, trying not to put a damper on the spirit of the night. Manny gave his wife a big smile, but made sure his plate contained at least one sample of each cookie. Carol simply shook her head and started filling the mugs which she handed to Sue to set on the table.

A few minutes later, as everyone was balancing full plates and hot drinks, Clark asked, "Hey Ted, how about a report on our neighborhood project. Have you learned anything new about how we can achieve our potential and enjoy life?"

Ted briefly reviewed the principles covered by the women at Alice's party plus the discussion with Manny, Carol, and Sue about rolling with the benefits. He also reviewed *YOU, NAPS* and *CHA*, then asked, "Maybe some of you can share how you applied one of these principles since the last time we were together."

Alice couldn't wait to speak. "You ladies were so encouraging at my first party. I've had five since then and the business is going very well. My two oldest kids are also involved. They help me process and handle the inventory. I think our working together is good for the family."

"So things are better with your teenage daughter?" Julie asked.

"Yes! That one idea about taking time to listen to her when she wants to talk — not necessarily when it's convenient for me — has paid off. She seems more relaxed just knowing I'm available when she needs me. The business has also helped give us more quality time together. In fact, Teri wants to put on a party for her friends and their mothers. I think it's a great idea, and I've agreed to let her have the proceeds from that party."

Carol reported that "rolling with the benefits" kept her from getting so uptight at work. "I'm more productive because I don't get frustrated when someone gives me a rush project. And Manny says I'm a little more relaxed when I get home. I'm enjoying life more because circumstances aren't frustrating me."

"I know I'm not as frustrated," added Sue. "Amy, that is such a freeing concept. I find I'm not resenting it as much when the kids change my plans. And the idea of planning things to do in different situations has made me more organized. By the way, we decided to let our kids go to bed at 10:00. We've had some great family times in the evening and it's no longer a hassle getting them to bed. And since they don't get up until 9:00, I have the time I need in the morning to get some things done."

Amy wanted to know if Robin had completed her computer course. "I have," she answered with a proud smile. "My boss really likes what I'm doing on the computer."

"Tell them what he wants to do," Angela prompted.

"I'm planning to take some community college classes at night. My boss wants me to do more study in computers and he'll pay for my schooling. He says he's thinking about putting our whole inventory record system on computer and when he does, he'd like me to train and supervise the keyboard operators."

"Congratulations!" The whole group was delighted at Robin's good news.

Angela was obviously proud of her roommate. "She never thought she could do something like this. Our neighborhood project has helped Robin see that she has a lot going for her. She's allowed herself to be stretched, and she's getting a promotion as a result."

"Sounds like the women have really gotten with the program," Sam chuckled.

"So what about you men?" Sue asked. "What have you been doing?"

There was an embarrassed silence for a moment. It wasn't that they weren't doing anything, but it took them a moment to think of specifics. Sam led off. "My relationship with the vice-president of marketing has improved slightly."

"That's good news. What made the difference?" Amy asked.

"Well, I've started listening to him more. One day not long ago, he got on me again about production. I felt like punching his lights out. Normally I would have just walked away. But I told myself, 'Sam, calm down. Try to understand.' So I took a few extra minutes and started asking him some questions about the pressure he was under. He talked about the frustration of getting a sales order and then having to delay delivery because production can't keep up with the demand. And then he said one of his kids had been sick and out of school for several weeks, and he was sorry that he had been a little testy. I think I got a new appreciation for his situation."

"Did you tell him your situation, too?" Ted asked.

"No, I think he knows how I feel. There wouldn't have been any point in that. What happened was that I didn't go back to my office all uptight like I usually do."

"That's progress," Ted affirmed. "Any other reports from the men?"

Manny referred to the conversation at Ted and Amy's a few weeks earlier. "I also like that idea of rolling with the benefits. The other day I was told I had to make an extra delivery and at first I resented the change in my schedule. Then I thought, 'Hey, what are the benefits?' For one thing, I'm getting some overtime pay and that's going to allow me to buy a new piece of photography equipment."

"Excuse me?" Carol interjected. "I think you mean buy some

things for the baby?"

"Well, uh, yeah, I guess we need to buy a crib." Several people smiled knowingly at the couple's exchange. Manny blushed, then quickly regained his composure. "Another positive was that they thought of me first; they could have asked someone else. So I decided it wasn't so bad."

"And before, you might have complained about the extra work?" Ted asked.

"Yeah, I'd have told my buddy Jose what a raw deal that was and we'd have talked down the company. But when I thought about some of the benefits, I didn't feel so bad about it."

"Clark, you've been quiet. How are you doing?"

"The one thing that's really helped me was your idea of doing my most unpleasant task first thing in the morning. Then it's done and the rest of the day is more enjoyable. That really works!" He was silent for a moment, but Ted and the others sensed he wasn't finished.

"You know, Ted, when we first met at your house, we talked about setting goals and so on. Well, as you know, I did that. You saw the objective statement I wrote. But to be honest with you, I haven't even looked at it for at least three months now. And Sam, we talked about organizing my desk . . . well, I started that night, and I installed that organizer you built for me. The new system worked great . . . for about two weeks. Now my desk is messier than ever. I guess my problem is that I'm not very disciplined. There are so many things and I can't seem to do them all."

"How many of you can relate to what Clark just said?" Ted asked. Everyone in the group nodded their heads and murmured agreement. "You see, you aren't alone. I have the same struggle myself. We all have great intentions. And we've all made some progress in different areas. But it is hard to follow through on all those great intentions. Let's talk about it for a minute. What can we do to encourage Clark?"

Angela spoke first. "I think Clark should take heart that he's making some progress. Since you're into sports, I'd say that making any major change in your life isn't like a sprint; it's more like a long-distance run. So persevere. Don't try to do it all at once."

"I think you called it the 'Swiss cheese' principle," Carol said. "You nibble away at it every day and put some holes in it."

"And keep at it until it's done," Amy added.

Angela thought of the example of Thomas Edison from her science background. "He defined genius as 98 percent perspiration and just two percent inspiration. When he was trying to perfect the light bulb he experimented with thousands of different filaments before he found the right one. It took years, but we're all grateful that he persevered."

"So if you want to fulfill your potential to the maximum, you need to stick with it," said Ted. "I think that's a crucial point. You need to follow through. But Clark, I sense you sometimes wonder if you'll ever make it in some of these areas." Clark nodded his head to indicate he agreed.

"I learned a very important lesson when I was a student at State," Ted continued. "I think it illustrates this point about pressing on even when the goal seems impossible. At State, everyone has to pass a water safety course in order to graduate. In that class we learned how to handle all kinds of situations in water, including what to do if we found ourselves in water with fire all around. To survive in that situation we would have to swim underwater. So one of the class objectives was to swim underwater the length of the pool and back. At the start of the term, all of us thought that was impossible.

"As the course progressed, we began to learn some techniques and pretty soon we realized it might be possible. Then in our final session, the instructor issued this challenge: If everyone in the class swam the length of the pool and back without coming up for air, everyone would get an A, no matter what else they had done that term. Well, I knew my limitations, so I got way back in the line; I didn't want to be the one who blew it for the whole class."

"But you didn't get back far enough," Sam chuckled.

"You got it! Everyone had made it when my turn came. Well, I determined I would make it or die trying. Fortunately, the instructor had warned us of all that we'd experience along the way. He said when we reached the point where we hurt so bad that we absolutely knew we couldn't go any further without air, we actually had nearly a minute left. So, I passed through that point and made it. Then wouldn't you know it, the next guy blew it!"

Everyone laughed at Ted's last statement. "All that for nothing!" Manny said.

"That's what I thought at first. But actually, it's become a great reminder of how much I can accomplish just through perseverance."

"Ted, I think that's a good point," Julie said. "But we can't do everything. I mean don't get me wrong; when you decide to do something, it's important to stay with it. But when do we stop and say, 'That's enough; I can't do any more'?"

"Can you give me a for instance?"

"Well, you know how full my calendar is. Right now, with the holidays, there are school programs, a special project with the Scouts, company and family parties . . . and then this afternoon my friend corners me and asks me to head up a special PTA committee. I felt

I couldn't let her down."

"Why not?" Alice asked.

"Well . . . because she's a friend and . . ."

"Julie, you're going to kill yourself," Sam said.

"You're an incredible person, but you can't do it all," Angela agreed.

"I know that. But, I guess I don't know how to say no."

"Would you like to learn?" said Ted with a gleam in his eye. "Perseverance does have its limitations. In order to say yes to some things, we have to say no to other things. Here's how we do it — I've learned this from hard experience. Everyone, clasp your hands in front of you like this and give me your best smile."

There were some chuckles at Ted's exaggerated pose and broad grin. Everyone except Sam copied him, clasping their hands. "C'mon, Sam, you can do it!" Manny kidded. Sam reluctantly complied.

"I see some of you don't have natural smiles," observed Ted. "Sleep with a coat hanger in your mouth and you'll have one by morning." That brought another round of laughs. "Now, everyone repeat after me. 'I'd lo-o-o-ve to do it. But, I can't.' " As he said "I can't," Ted unclasped his hands and made a motion with them like he was gently shoving a heavy object away from him.

There was more laughter, but Ted ignored it and said, "C'mon, let's help Julie here. All together now: 'I'd lo-o-ove to do it. But I can't.' "

"I'd lo-o-ove to do it. But I can't," the group chorused and motioned with their hands.

"Not bad. Let's do it one more time . . ." This time, everyone participated enthusiastically. "That's really good. Now Julie, you need to practice. Say no at least once a day this next week. OK?"

Julie, with a smile of relief, promised she would.

Robin mentioned that she had learned to use the principle of saying no in another way. "Alice, you were the one who gave me the idea. I don't have a lot of commitments like Julie, but I found I was wasting more time than I wanted to. Things like watching too much TV, just leafing through magazines, socializing too long, or just daydreaming. I believe there's an appropriate time for each of those activities, but sometimes I use them as escapes from what I should be doing. That's when I need to say no and do something more productive."

"You're not saying it's bad to watch TV or read a magazine," Angela wanted to clarify.

"Not at all. But it has to be balanced. If I'm to reach my potential, I have a lot to learn. I can spend some of the time I might have spent reading a magazine by perhaps starting to explore some of the materials for the classes I'll be taking at the community college."

"Something else you've done is make yourself accountable. When you told me you wanted to make better use of your time, you wanted me to ask occasionally how you're doing."

"Yes, that's helped. It's not that Angela checks up on me all the time. If I'm watching TV, she doesn't say, 'Shouldn't you be reading a good book?' But realizing that she knows my goals helps me be more diligent in working toward those goals."

"I think we all need something like that," Clark said. "At our company I call it the day of reckoning, when we have our developmental review. I know every six months my performance will be evaluated, and that helps me do more than I might otherwise."

"That's a valid point," Ted agreed. "Let's be honest, most of us don't like having our work inspected. But it does help us do better work."

Sue brought out the fact that even in a family, some accountability is built in. "Clark and I talk about our kids and how we're going to handle different situations. That helps our discipline. It would be easy to let down and not follow through in a situation, except I know Clark and I have agreed on a certain approach — so I do it."

"I wish there was something like that in some of my volunteer projects," Julie complained. "I tell you, some of the mothers, they'll say you can count on them for something, and then the day comes and nothing. It drives me crazy."

"Discipline. That's what we need," Sam said. To him, it was all cut and dried. He ignored his wife's annoyed look.

"What do you mean by that?" Carol asked.

"I think I know what he means," Angela said. "If something is important and you really want to do it, then *do* it. Don't just sit around talking about it."

"Yes — but it's not that simple," Clark protested. "Sometimes it's awfully hard to get going."

"So how do we handle that?" asked Ted.

"Have any of you ever heard of the Polar Bear Club?" Alice asked. "They're a group of people who go swimming in Lake Michigan every winter."

"They're crazy!"

"I won't argue with that. But I was talking with someone who belonged to that group. You know how they get in? They don't dip their toes or splash a little water on their chests. They get in as fast as they can. They take the plunge."

"Before they change their minds," Clark laughed.

"That's the idea. I think what Angela's saying is that there are some things that we just don't like doing. If we're disciplined, sometimes the best thing to do is just start . . . *get going.*"

"It's interesting that once you get started, it isn't so bad," Angela continued. "In fact, five minutes after I start I usually *feel* like doing it."

Ted pressed the issue further. "But, let's be honest, there are some things we may never like doing. I know at work I try to do some of those unpleasant tasks during dead spots when I might not do anything else. For example, say I've got ten minutes before lunch. Rather than waste that time, I could make the phone call I've been putting off. The point is that I can bear almost anything when I know it will be over in ten minutes."

"The best way to get me to do something I don't want to do is schedule a meeting on it," Sam said. "Then I'm on the hook and I'll get it done."

Sam's wife agreed. "The fact is, sometimes we just have to rise above our feelings or we'll never achieve our potential. So if I've made a commitment to the Scouts or PTA, I'll get it done regardless."

Amy referred to the discussion the women had had at Alice's. "Discipline relates to thinking through what we're going to do, making a decision, then planning the follow-through. I think it's easier to do those unpleasant tasks when we've explored the alternatives and made our decision. We may not like the one task, but it's only a small part of the desirable objective we want to reach. That gives perspective to the individual task."

Ted offered another idea. "Sometimes a little reward helps. One thing I don't enjoy about my job is writing reports. I'd much rather give a talk or meet with some of our sales staff. Nevertheless, I have to write reports. Often I tell myself, 'When you finish this report, you can take a coffee break at Brenner's.' That's the donut shop half a block from my office. The promise of that reward helps me write the report."

"There's also a negative incentive," Clark said. "Right before we moved here, I lost an important account because I was slow writing up an order. As you know, I hate paperwork, but I hate losing a sale even more. So I do it. Of course, you have all helped me see that I can do it even more efficiently."

"There's one other point about discipline," Amy said. "I used to be a compulsive house cleaner. Unless every speck of dust was removed, it wasn't clean. Now I was disciplined in cleaning house, and I still am, but I found that my standard was too high. I was wasting too much time cleaning every nook and cranny. There were other more important things to do with my time. So now I clean house once a week and before company comes, but I don't worry about it being spotless."

"Sounds like a matter of balance," said Julie.

Ted agreed. "I learned an important principle in business school and I think it's true universally. In most situations, 80 percent of the desired result is accomplished in 20 percent of the time. The perfectionist needs to realize that sometimes it isn't worth going to the 100 percent level because 80 percent will often accomplish the purpose. That was certainly the case with Amy and cleaning house. The way I look at it, she's closer to fulfilling her potential doing four things to the 80 percent level than one to the 100 percent level. Doing that last 20 percent in house cleaning was an awful waste of her time and talents."

"Perhaps that's part of saying no," Amy concluded. "I had to say no to my high standards in that area. I've done the same thing with Ted's den. I wish he'd sort through all his magazines and files and throw most of the stuff out. But he's helped me realize that it's a better use of his time just to add a file cabinet or two and keep the clutter somewhat organized."

"The cost of file cabinets or boxes is cheap compared to the time and effort I'd need to go through each file item by item. So I'll worry about it when I run out of space, and that won't be for many years."

"How about some more cookies and cider," Carol suggested. Several people stirred, so Ted decided it was time to wrap up the discussion.

"This really has been most enlightening. We could go on, I'm sure, and come up with many more ideas. I'd like to summarize quickly what I think we've said. In three words."

"I can't believe this guy," Sam laughed.

"Got it in a neat little acrostic for us?" Clark asked.

"Yes, as a matter of fact I do. *PAD*. I think most everything we've said tonight could be summarized by three key concepts."

FOLLOW-THROUGH

- **P**ERSISTENCE—Keep at the important things until you're done
- **A**CCOUNTABILITY—"Report" to someone
- **D**ISCIPLINE—Implement despite feelings

"That's it, all right!" Alice said. Everyone agreed.

Several people rose and gathered again around the table for a final cookie or two before heading home. Angela put her arm around Carol. "Great party. Thanks for having us over."

Sam and Julie cornered Ted and Amy before they could leave. "Ah, Ted, I was wondering if you . . ." Sam hesitated, as though something was caught in his throat.

"We'd like to spend a little time with you," Julie said. "You two seem to communicate so well, and we thought maybe you wouldn't mind sharing a few tips."

Amy glanced at Ted, then at the Turners. "We'd love to. Let's schedule a time right after Christmas." As Sam and Julie left, Ted thought about how they seemed to be learning. They really wanted to have a successful marriage. But their communication was obviously strained. He hoped that he and Amy could help them improve in that area so they could achieve their potential and enjoy life more as a married couple.

*How you can tell others what
you feel and think in a clear,
positive way.*

8

SPEAKING YOUR MIND

The Turners were in a serious mood during dinner at the Simpsons. It's not that they didn't enjoy the social time — they did. But they were concerned about their marriage. Ted and Amy sensed the tension and felt it was important to make this time positive as well as helpful.

Amy referred to the Christmas party when Sam had talked about the relationship with the vice president of marketing. "Any new developments there?" she asked.

"Not really. During the holidays, we kind of slow down. I haven't even seen him for a week. I did hear he had to put his son in the hospital for two days to run some tests."

"Have you expressed any concern to him about that?" asked Ted.

"No. I haven't. I guess I should."

Sam was quiet, musing on the thought.

"I will say that Sam has done some thoughtful things for me in recent weeks," Julie said. "I told the ladies about how he's listened to me . . . it's been on several occasions now. I feel like he's understanding me better. The day before Christmas, he brought me some beautiful flowers; that was a real surprise. And last week, we had a special night out. He took me to my favorite restaurant and then to a show I've wanted to see. I really appreciated that."

"It sounds like you're making progress on caring and listening," Ted observed. "Those were two things we discussed at our picnic in September. How about the third area — affirming or encouraging?"

Sam shook his head. "I guess I'm not too good at that."

"Maybe we can help you. It's something we can all learn to do better."

"Sam, have you thought of the people you most enjoy being around?" Amy asked. "For instance, how do you feel when someone makes a negative remark to you or about you?"

"Well, I don't like it. I feel down, or sometimes I'm mad or defensive."

"When someone makes a positive remark to you, do you feel good?"

"Well, yes."

"As good as you felt bad in the earlier example?"

"No, not really."

"I think that's true for most people. In fact, research has shown that it takes five or more of those positive affirmations to compensate emotionally for one negative statement or criticism."

"Think about that with our kids," Ted reflected. "It's so easy to pick on the negative and never notice all the positive things they do."

"But who's going to correct them if we only notice the positives?"

"Good point — we can't ignore what they're doing wrong. As good parents, we must correct them. But we need to balance that with encouragement. Your son, Ken, demonstrated the power of encouragement with the story about his PE class."

"If it's so powerful with kids, or in a PE class," said Amy, "then that tells me how important it is with a spouse. I know I need to hear Ted tell me that he loves me, and that he likes how I look, and that he appreciates the meal I've fixed. Then when he does have to talk about something that's perhaps a criticism, it's not so threatening. I know he supports me."

Sam heaved a sigh and said, "I know what you're saying is true. Julie is such a good woman. We have our spats, but overall . . ."

Ted probed a little. "Can you be a little more specific? What do you like about her?"

"Well . . ." He shrugged his shoulders.

Ted looked over at Julie, and again noticed her beauty. "For one thing, if you don't mind my saying so, Julie's very attractive."

Julie glanced at Ted with a combination of appreciation and slight embarrassment. Sam nodded in agreement. "You bet. I married a 'good looker.' "

"So what do you like about her appearance?"

"Oh, several things — her hair is always so nice."

"Tell Julie!"

"And I really like that red dress, the one you wore to the banquet a few months ago. You looked so pretty in it."

Julie laughed. "I thought you *didn't* like it. That's why I haven't worn it since."

"Keep going," Ted encouraged. "Can you think of something else?"

"I've always liked the fact that you always look so sharp, even when you're not dressed up." Sam stopped for a moment but Ted could tell he was thinking. "You're such a good cook. Especially lasagna. You make the best lasagna."

"I'll make some tomorrow!" Julie said with a growing smile.

"Don't stop now," Amy prompted Sam.

"You know what I really appreciate is how you're so good with the kids. You really work at knowing their teachers, and you get involved in their club activities. I don't see how any mother could do more than you do with our children."

Julie reached out and grabbed her husband's hand. "Thanks, honey. I appreciate that."

"How do you feel?" Ted asked Sam.

"OK. I guess it wasn't so bad once I got going."

"That's what's so good about affirming and encouraging people. It makes us feel good as well as the person we're talking to."

"Like anything, it takes practice," Amy added. "Ted has learned to give me lots of encouragement, and I need it when I've spent a day with the kids or had a full schedule of teaching piano. But I know Ted needs it, too. He's appreciated at work, but he also needs my encouragement."

"You know, this is good," Julie said, with some hesitation. "But there's a deeper problem." She pushed her plate forward and rested her arms on the edge of the table. "Sam's been much better at listening to me lately, but I can't get him to tell me what's on his mind. For example, I know he's not happy at work. But he won't talk about it. Outside of what I've heard him tell you about the one vice president, I really don't know what's going on in his job. Is he thinking of quitting? Does he want to change jobs within the company? Will that mean a move? I'm afraid he might come home some day and say he just quit."

Sam shifted in his chair, obviously uncomfortable again. But he knew he and Julie needed help, so he didn't protest. Julie continued, "I guess you know we've both been married before. My first husband

and I just drifted apart. I didn't know he was upset until one day he just up and left. I just can't stand the thought of going through that again."

Amy mentioned an article she had read recently. "It said that a study of more than one hundred couples who experienced marital problems showed that in every case criticism was a major factor. In more than half of those cases, both husband and wife were very critical of each other. I think the reason that's a problem is because constant criticism wears you down, especially if that's the primary form of communication. That doesn't mean we don't talk about problems. But when we talk about them in a spirit of mutual encouragement — rather than criticism — they're not nearly so threatening.

"Let me give you an example. Ted, do you remember our conversation last Sunday after church?"

Ted nodded his head, slightly surprised his wife would bring up that incident.

"Sometimes I have a problem being on time. And Ted is *always* on time; early if possible. Well, we were late for church last Sunday for the second week in a row. Ted could have criticized me, but he didn't. He did tell me how he felt — he really didn't like it. But he said, 'Can we find a way to solve this problem?' So I knew what he was thinking, yet because he handled it so well, we were able to talk calmly about a solution. We decided I'd get up fifteen minutes earlier on Sunday mornings, and Ted would do a couple more things to help get the kids ready."

Sam appreciated the example. "My problem is that I've always had a hard time saying what's on my mind. I mean, I know what I want to say, but I just can't seem to get it out."

"What holds you back?" Ted asked.

"I guess I don't like being misunderstood. Many times when I do speak, it seems like the other person reacts or doesn't understand what I really mean. So I don't say anything and the frustration builds until finally I just blurt something out." With a resigned laugh, he added, "Then everyone's upset."

"That is a common problem," Amy said. "Many times people don't know how to organize their thoughts and express them in a way that would be easily understood without creating unnecessary emotion."

"Would it help if there were some way to plan your communication," Ted asked, "so you could express something major you want to say without upsetting the person you're talking to?"

"I guess it would."

"Then let me suggest a process — again, learned in the school of hard knocks. If you want to say something important to Julie and you feel you're stuck — you just can't seem to get it out — then take a couple of minutes to plan it. Remember what Alice taught us about how she applied her decision by asking *What, how,* and *when?* Let's elaborate on that and use it to help us plan what we're going to say.

"So, you've decided you need to tell Julie something. The first thing is to ask yourself *What and why.* What do you want to say, and why do you want to say it? For example, *what* I wanted to tell Amy last Sunday was that she needed to be ready for church earlier. The *why* was because I didn't like arriving late, trying to find a place to park in a crowded parking lot, then rushing into the sanctuary and creating a distraction because the service has already started.

"Next I ask *Who?* To whom am I talking?"

"Isn't that obvious?" Julie asked. "You're talking to your wife."

"Yes, that's obvious. But by thinking of *who* I'm recognizing that Amy is different from you, Julie. Or from my boss. Or from my three children. Or, most important, from me. I can't tell her the same way I might tell someone else. I need to know her moods, how she thinks . . . I need to *understand* her. Like many artistic people, Amy is sensitive. Some people don't mind criticism. Others can't handle it without a lot of affirmation. My wife needs to know that I support her. She needs to be spoken to gently, and with lots of encouragement."

"You can't just come out and say what's on your mind?" Sam asked.

"That *is* what I want to do. But I want to make sure the communication is as clear to her when she receives it as it is to me when I send it. If I hurt her feelings at the start, then it's much harder for her to hear my message. And unfortunately in many marriages today there is so much negative emotional baggage that it's very difficult to communicate even simple messages."

"But surely you don't need to worry about every word?"

"If I need to inform Amy that I'm going to the store, I'll probably just say, 'Amy, I'm going to the store. I'll be back in ten minutes.' But if it's something to which she might react emotionally, or something that's important to me and I want to be sure she understands how I feel, then I need to tailor my approach to how she thinks and responds.

"Next I need to consider the *How.* How am I going to say it? And finally *When.* Sometimes timing is important. For example, when I get home from work and Amy is trying to fix dinner, that is not the time for a serious discussion. Or, as she's said, she doesn't function well late at night. So after 9:00 is not a good time to talk about an important issue. For us, we've found that going out for breakfast on Saturday morning is often an excellent time to talk."

Sam shook his head. "That's a lot to remember."

"What and why, who, how, and when. Maybe it would help if Amy and I gave you a little demonstration. Honey, do you remember the discussion we had recently about Nancy?"

"Yes, that's a good example," Amy said. "This was a positive situation, but it was also important. One evening, I told Ted I'd like to have breakfast so we could talk about our daughter's plans for the summer."

"So two days later, we went to breakfast. Notice Amy thought out when it would be best to talk about this, rather than springing a big item on me that evening. We'll give you an idea of how our conversation went."

Amy began the re-creation of their dialogue. "Ted, Nancy's violin teacher says she is doing extremely well. In fact, she says Nancy is probably the best student she's ever had. She thinks we should consider sending Nancy to a special camp this summer for three weeks where she can get some advanced training and experience."

"What does Nancy think?"

"She really wants to do it. But we also talked about how she had planned to work this summer to help pay some of the cost for college this fall. She's afraid that taking three weeks off in mid-summer might cost her a job and that might jeopardize her plans for school."

"We're still waiting to hear about two scholarship applications that she's made. If she wins one of them, that might relieve some of the financial burden."

"If that doesn't happen, I still think we should consider if there's some way we can arrange this for Nancy. She needs to find out how far she can go with her violin and this is an outstanding opportunity."

"I agree. If there is a way we can do it, we should. How soon will we need to make a decision?"

"She needs to begin the application process now. But we've got several weeks before we have to make a final decision — if she's even accepted into the program."

"Then let's discuss it with Nancy and encourage her to apply for the program. Meanwhile, we can study our financial options."

Amy turned to Sam and Julie. "End of demonstration. Notice we weren't making any decisions at this point. We were exchanging information. I told Ted the situation and what I thought. Ted asked some questions, listened to me, then told me what he thought. I didn't assume I knew what Ted was thinking; he didn't assume he knew what I was thinking. Our open communication laid the foundation for us to make a good decision when that time comes."

"Amy knew what she wanted to say and why," Ted explained. "She determined the best way to do this was in a relaxed manner, over breakfast, when I could give her my full attention and ask questions."

Sam cleared his throat. "There is something I've been wanting to tell Julie."

"Don't say anything yet!" Ted cautioned, as he held up a hand. "Before you tell Julie anything, let's go into the living room for a minute and plan what you're going to say. Ladies, I hope you don't mind visiting for a moment while Sam prepares."

Julie offered to help Amy clear the table. As the women stacked the dishes, the men moved into the living room where Ted asked Sam to tell him what he wanted to say. "Julie's right about my not being happy at work. I've wanted to tell her that I'd like to explore the possibility of starting my own business — building cabinets and furniture. But I don't know what she'd think of the idea. It'd be risky as far as my income is concerned."

"Has Julie ever indicated, by her words or attitude, that she doesn't want you to be happy in life?"

"No. No, actually, I guess she's been pretty supportive."

"Does she have a lifestyle that would be adversely affected by the kind of a change you're exploring?"

"No, we live rather modestly. Julie handles our budget and she never wastes anything. I wouldn't call her a social climber."

"Then what are you worried about?"

"I don't know. I guess it's the risk . . ."

The men talked for a few minutes and then called the women into the living room. "OK, Sam, go for it," Ted gently encouraged.

"Honey, I feel you've always wanted me to do what I really enjoy doing."

"I hope I've communicated that," Julie answered, looking intently into her husband's face. "I do want you to be happy."

"Well, you probably know I'm not happy in my job."

"Yes, but I don't know the details."

"Well, I've been doing a lot of thinking. This isn't something we should do immediately, but someday I'd like to get out of my job and start a business making furniture and cabinets."

Julie smiled. "You'd really enjoy that, wouldn't you?"

"I love working with wood. And everyone says my work is high quality, and there seems to be a market for my furniture. I'm not saying I should quit my job, but I'm wondering if I should start seriously developing this business, so that maybe someday, a year or two or three from now, I could quit my job and make a living at it."

"Sam, if that's what you really want to do, I think you ought to start working toward that dream."

"There's a lot of unanswered questions. I have good benefits at the company. We'd have to make adjustments."

"Well, I think I'd be willing to help you see if it can work out."

"We don't have to make a decision right now. I just wanted you to know what I was thinking." Sam suddenly broke into a grin, as if a weight had been lifted off his shoulders. He turned to Ted and asked, "How did I do?"

Ted and Amy both clapped enthusiastically. "Great job, Sam!" Amy said. She noticed that Julie's eyes were moist.

"It's not so bad once you say it. I guess I was afraid of what Julie might think."

"But Sam, it's worse when I don't know what you're thinking! How can I help you if I don't know?"

"Well, now it's out in the open and we can talk about it, even if it never happens."

"That's right," Ted said. "And your communication will get easier with practice. Let me suggest that at least once a week you ought to schedule some time just to talk like this, with both of you sharing what's on your mind."

"That way things don't build up," Amy added. "Sometimes Ted and I get so busy that we just need a time away — over dinner or breakfast, or on a walk — just to talk."

"There is something else I've been meaning to tell you," Ted said, and the Turners laughed as he said it, realizing he was practicing what he'd just taught them. "Seriously, we've talked about how to tell each other what we're thinking. But there is another element in our marriage that has made a very significant difference in our relationship. In fact, it's the foundation for our marriage and our family . . ."

A siren interrupted. The four of them heard the emergency vehicle tear down Jackson Avenue and turn onto Fir Court, sounding as if it were going to drive right into the living room. After sitting frozen for a moment, the two couples jumped to their feet and rushed to the front door. An ambulance, its lights flashing in the dark night, had stopped next door in front of the home of Bob and Ginny Harris.

* * *

It was midnight and Ted was writing in his notebook. The paramedics had spent nearly forty-five minutes working on Bob, who had suffered a heart attack.

They had finally moved him into the ambulance and Ginny had climbed aboard. Several of the neighbors had stood outside with the Turners and Simpsons and watched. Then, with few comments, they returned to their homes. Sam and Julie thanked the Simpsons for the evening and headed home.

The emergency had shocked Ted and Amy and they said little as they cleaned up the kitchen. Just being together right now was enough. When Amy headed for bed, Ted said he wanted to write down his thoughts and that he'd join her in a moment.

Ted thought about the evening with the Turners and was pleased that Sam was so open to coaching. If the Turners could refine their relationship and communication skills, there was a lot of potential for that marriage. And what were these skills? Ted reviewed the earlier *CHA* acrostic he had developed under the heading, "Enjoy Quality Relationships." Then he added a last point, *Tell:*

ENJOY "QUALITY" RELATIONSHIPS

- **C** ARE—Let people know they are important
- **H** EAR—Listen until you understand
- **A** FFIRM—Let people know they are doing well
- **T** ELL—Communicate clearly and sensitively

Then he elaborated on *Tell*.

TELL—COMMUNICATE CLEARLY AND SENSITIVELY

- **W** HAT do you want to say?
- **W** HY do you want to say it?
- **W** HO are you talking to?
- **H** OW should you best present it?
- **W** HEN should you say it?

Ted put his notebook away and joined his wife in bed. Amy was still awake. "I can't get over it," she said as she cuddled up to her husband. "On the one hand, we knew Bob wasn't that well. Yet it's still such a shock. Poor Ginny."

"We need to reach out and offer help," Ted whispered. "At times like this I feel so inadequate. I guess it will never be easy."

"At least we can pray."

They were quiet for a moment as they each silently prayed for their next-door neighbors. Then Ted said, "This is a shock to the whole neighborhood. We need to pull together."

"And offer *hope*. There will be a chance to talk to Sam and Julie again soon. What you were going to say is really the key not just to their marriage. It is also the key to our ability to handle this crisis."

When the bottom falls out,
where can you find hope and
peace that sustains you?

9

THE SEARCH FOR PEACE

The word spread quickly through the neighborhood. Amy learned it by phone. "I called to see if you'd heard the news," Angela reported.

"What news?"

"Bob passed away about three hours ago. I just stopped by the hospital to check on Ginny and that's how I found out."

Amy was shocked but managed to ask, "How is she doing?"

"I haven't seen her. I think she's with the mortician."

"I don't believe it. He seemed to be improving when we saw him last night. I thought he'd pull through."

"Apparently he had another heart attack and this time it was too much."

"OK, Angela. I appreciate this. Would you like me to call the others in our neighborhood?"

"I'll help. I'll call Julie and Alice if you'll call Sue and Carol."

Amy called Sue first, then Carol, who began to cry while she was on the phone. "Would you like to come over and talk?"

"Yes," Carol said as she tried to gain some composure. "I'll be right there."

Carol was still dressed in the gray suit she had worn to work. Manny was away for a couple of days on a long run, so Carol appreciated the invitation. As soon as she sat on the couch, the tears started flowing again. Amy went over and put an arm around Carol. After a few minutes she went to the kitchen and brought back a box of tissues. Carol gratefully accepted one.

"I'm sorry," she said. "I'm surprised how hard this has hit me."

"It's OK to cry. I'm so glad you came over."

Carol blew her nose, then began to tell Amy about Manny. "He's overweight, as you know. Well, he's not really fat, but he loves to eat. His father died of a heart attack when Manny was just a kid. His family has a history of heart attacks. I tell him to be careful of what he eats, but . . ." Carol shook her head, then dried off her tears.

"I guess I see Ginny and feel so sorry for her . . . then I think that could be me," Carol continued. "How old was her husband? Fifty-five? Manny's gone so much and now with the baby coming, I worry about his safety on the road. And I worry about his health. I know I shouldn't worry so much, but I can't seem to help it. I've even had a couple of nightmares . . . the kind where I'm a widow and I have my little baby and Manny's not there . . ." She leaned back and said, "You probably think I'm foolish for telling you this."

"Not at all. I've felt some similar kinds of emotions. It's not unusual to have such thoughts."

"You seem to have it all together. I don't see you worried or uptight."

Amy laughed a gentle laugh, then sat down on the chair right next to the couch and looked Carol in the eye. "Maybe I hide it better than you," she said with a smile. "I'll admit I do have a few years of experience. However, I have also learned how to deal with my worries in a very positive way." She stopped to see if Carol was interested. Her friend was glued to every word. "The turning point for me was when my father died ten years ago after a bout with cancer. Would you like me to tell you about it?"

Carol nodded her head. "Please do."

Just then, the ladies heard Ted's car pull into the driveway. As Ted got out of his car, he saw Sam step out of his front door and holler, "Did you hear the news?"

"What's up?"

Sam walked across the street and met Ted on the sidewalk in front of his house. "Bob died this afternoon."

"Oh no! I didn't know. Amy probably tried to call, but I was out of the office."

Sam leaned on Ted's car and shook his head. "Julie just told me a few minutes ago. He seemed like a good man, though I never really got to know him."

"None of us did. I had a couple of very short talks with him. You know, just about the weather, that kind of thing."

"His wife is nice. But I don't think they had many friends." Sam shook his head. "It's sad."

A gust of cold wind reminded them that it was still winter. Ted invited Sam to come in for some coffee, and Sam accepted. "Julie's working with a couple of kids in the scout troop. We'll be eating a late dinner after they're gone."

Amy had just started her story when Sam and Ted entered the house. She stopped and asked if they'd heard the news.

"Sam just told me," Ted answered. He noticed Carol and how her eyes were red from crying. "Are you all right?"

"It hit Carol hard. I was just starting to tell her about my father."

"Sam and I will go to the family room . . ."

"No, it's OK," Carol said. "I don't mind if you join us."

Sam sat down respectfully as Ted went into the kitchen to heat some water for tea and coffee. Amy reviewed what she'd said for Sam's benefit. "We were discussing our fear of death. I was just telling Carol about the time my father died, about ten years ago. I can still remember how devastated I was when I got the news. Just a month before, my father learned he had cancer, and before I could get home to see him, he was gone. There was so little time to prepare.

"My parents lived about a thousand miles away. Of course I flew back to be with the family and I stayed with my mom. As you might imagine, she was heartbroken. But she wasn't devastated. I was the one who did most of the crying, and she tried to comfort me. For the first time, I noticed how solid her life was. She was at peace and had a sense of hope. Several times she said to me, 'I miss your father, but I'm going to see him again someday.' "

Amy looked at Carol and Sam to check their reactions. They were listening intently. Ted came in quietly and set tea on the table in front of Amy and Carol, then handed Sam a cup of coffee.

Amy continued: "Faith in God was an important part of our lives. At a young age, I thought I had become a Christian. But I guess I never really understood what that meant. My folks, while they were very committed to their faith and set a good example, never talked a lot about it. So as I grew up and left home I didn't take my spiritual life very seriously. Now, however, as I saw my mother's reaction to my dad's death and compared it to my reaction, I realized she had something very different from what I had.

"I'll never forget the funeral service. The speaker talked about the hope and peace of mind we can have in Christ. As he talked, I realized I really didn't have that hope and peace. Afterward, I talked to him privately and he was very understanding. He took the time to show me how I could have that hope in God through Jesus Christ. It really was quite simple as I think back on it. I asked Christ to forgive me for the many ways in which I had fallen far short of His expectations of me. I also asked Him to come into my life, to help me live my life in the way in which He would be pleased. And as I did, I sensed a tremendous peace. I knew this was the kind of peace my mom had. Over the next few days, I also began to sense the same hope my mom had, that I would see my father again some-day in heaven."

It was quiet for a moment and everyone could hear the sounds of several kids outside playing a rowdy game of football under the street lights. Carol broke the silence by asking, "Did that peace and hope stay with you?"

"Yes. It's been ten years and it's never left. Excuse me — I should say that there are moments when I feel anxiety, but when I go back to God and ask Him to give me His peace, within a short time I again feel that special calm from Him."

Carol nodded her head as she thought about what she'd just heard. Sam asked Ted if he noticed any difference in his wife.

Ted gave a gentle chuckle. "I'll say I did. She was a different person. Amy used to be a big worrier. She worried about the kids, about how the house looked, about what the neighbors thought, about her husband not saying dumb things when we had company. I'd try to tell her that worrying didn't change anything, but my advice never helped."

"It used to bug me when Ted would say, 'Don't worry.' I couldn't not worry. But after I asked Christ to come into my life, that began to change. For example, a few months after my father's death, our oldest child Nancy became very ill. At first, doctors thought she had spinal meningitis. Carol, I think I understand some of your fears — all kinds of horrible thoughts race through your mind. I was an emotional wreck. I remember just praying about my fears and telling God how much I loved my daughter and didn't want to lose her. And as I did that, I soon had His peace again. Fortunately, they ran some more tests and discovered it wasn't so serious. She was in the hospital a couple of days and then was sent home. But even though this situation turned out well, I learned how real God's presence can be in difficult situations."

Ted took the story from there. "After that, I think one of the things that made a difference in Amy was that she began to be satisfied with what she had in life. She's a very talented woman, and she's a perfectionist. While she's never stopped striving to be the best she can be, she's come to accept the fact that she can't, for example, be the world's best piano player."

"Ted, honey, I don't think I ever wanted to be the best piano player in the world. But I did want to be the best I could possibly be. I set lofty goals and I won awards for my playing. My frustration lay in the fact that I never was satisfied when I achieved those goals. I began to wonder if anything would satisfy me. I remember winning a regional competition in college when I was a junior. It was a prestigious piano contest and I was the first person from my college to win it. But even as I received the award, I was asking myself, 'What's the big deal?' I couldn't really enjoy it. So I began thinking that maybe marriage would satisfy me. But much as I loved Ted, that still didn't seem like enough. Neither was teaching, or having kids. After I became a Christian, I realized that *Christ* was a tremendous source of satisfaction, regardless of my circumstances. That allowed me to relax and enjoy whatever I was doing. Whether I did well or not, I could have peace and satisfaction."

"You asked if I noticed a difference," Ted gestured to Sam. "It was like night and day. We had gone to church occasionally but when Amy came back after her father's funeral, we started going every Sunday. I really didn't mind that; I thought it might provide more contacts for my insurance business."

Sam smiled at Ted's honesty. "I hadn't thought about that. People join civic clubs for the same reason."

"Then Amy started going to a Bible study, and she asked me to go, too. Now I didn't mind church, and I thought it was good that Amy was going to the Bible study. After all, she needed it — she was the one who worried so much. But I was a successful businessman. I was moving up in the company. I didn't need a crutch, and I didn't want her pushing me. And she didn't. She went to her Bible study and I noticed that she wasn't as uptight about things. Occasionally she'd invite me to go to the study, but there was never any pressure. Finally one week I went, thinking that this would satisfy her and she'd stop asking me.

"The study was held in a home, and I was surprised to find that there were a lot of young couples our age in the group. The men weren't losers like I thought they would be. So I began to think maybe this wasn't so bad after all. Later that week I had lunch with Jack, the Bible study leader, and he talked to me about how we are multi-dimensional beings. There are the physical, emotional, and intellectual parts, but there is also the spiritual dimension. We need all four to be complete. Many people develop the first three, but ignore the spiritual.

"Here's what really got my attention. He said that we can never achieve our God-given potential if we ignore the spiritual dimension of our lives. I'd never considered that. Then he gave me a little booklet — which I want to give you in a moment. I read it that night. It explained how I could come alive spiritually.

"As I read through that booklet, I realized that while I was considered a moral and upright man in the community, I wasn't pleasing God. I mean I was trying to be a good person, trying to realize my potential, but God's desire for my life was so far beyond that. It was staggering. He has a totally different standard. It was late and Amy was asleep when I asked God to forgive me for going my own way. Then I asked Christ to come into my life and make me the kind of person *He* wanted me to be."

"My husband didn't change dramatically right away," Amy explained. "He was always committed to me and the family. But I think his priorities changed. He became more interested in people rather than just making sales. He wanted people to succeed, to achieve their full potential — that's when that desire really developed. And it carried over into our spiritual lives. He wanted all of us in the family to reach our spiritual potential."

"That's why Amy and I continued to go to the study each week. I *wanted* to go now. One week, we studied a story where Christ taught that it is very important to make the most of what we've been given. The story was about how three men were given different amounts of money. Two of the men invested well and doubled their money. The other didn't do anything. The point was that God expects us to be all that we can be with what He has given us.

"That lesson jolted me. It made me realize that I have a responsibility to use *all* that God has given me — whether it's my abilities, finances, possessions, whatever. That's when I formulated a life-long objective — to achieve my potential and to help others achieve theirs."

"That affected our whole family," Amy continued. "Ted really became less selfish. Like I said, he was committed to the family, but now he became more active. He wasn't just spending time with us, but he was actively looking for ways to love me and the kids."

Ted and Amy were quiet for a moment, allowing their friends to reflect on what they'd said. Suddenly, the Simpsons' youngest child burst into the house, his nose bloodied from the football game in the street. Amy grabbed the box of tissues and jumped up to comfort the crying boy.

Sam checked his watch and realized he needed to head home. "Julie's going to have dinner on any minute. Thanks for inviting me in. You've given me a lot to think about."

"If you can hold on one moment, I'll get that booklet I

mentioned," Ted said. When he returned, he gave booklets to Sam and Carol.* "If you want, we can talk more about this later, after you've read it," he said to Sam.

"Yes, I definitely would be interested in talking some more."

Then Sam left and Carol said, "I probably should go, too, so you can take care of your boy." The child had stopped crying but Amy continued to hold him in her arms and comfort him. "Thank you for being so understanding, and for taking the time. It really has helped."

"Any time you want to talk, please feel free to come over. I want to encourage you to know that there is an answer for our fears."

"Thank you so much for talking with me. I can really see how your faith has helped you deal with worry. You've given me a lot to think about." As Carol prepared to go out the door, she said, "You know, I wish there were some way we could help Ginny. She's got to be feeling so lonely and worried."

"I agree. She has a son, but I don't know if she has any other family."

"Do you think she'd mind if we brought over meals for a few days?"

"That's an excellent idea! I'm sure she won't want to be concerned about cooking."

"I'll call the ladies on our block and see if maybe each of us can take a meal over during the next week."

"Count me in," said Amy. "Let me know what evening is not covered and I'll take that one."

---

* See appendix C for the text of the booklet Ted gave to Sam and Carol.

*Three powerful ways to deal
with the anxiety that robs your
energy.*

10

STRATEGIES
TO HANDLE WORRY

Ginny's home was tastefully decorated with antiques. It was obvious that she had carefully studied and selected her purchases over the years. Figurines and hand-crocheted doilies graced the coffee and lamp tables.

Carol and Angela had come over to check on their neighbor. Carol was bringing a meal. "Would you like to stay a few minutes?" Ginny asked. "I'll heat some water for tea." The women sensed Ginny wanted to talk and accepted her invitation.

"I can't believe all the food people have brought over," Ginny said as she put down a plate of banana bread. "This came from Alice. I can't possibly eat it all."

"Glad to help!" Angela laughed as she accepted a slice. Of all the neighbors, she was the most relaxed with Ginny.

Ginny poured the hot water into a pot, dropped three tea bags in it, then put the pot in a cozy and placed it on the coffee table to steep.

"How are you doing?" Carol asked tentatively.

"Oh, about as well as can be expected," Ginny sighed. "My son went back home two days ago. He's so busy. Owns a business and really can't be away from it for long . . ." Her voice trailed off.

"You're feeling the loneliness now, aren't you?" Angela probed gently.

The women saw Ginny's eyes well up with tears, but she controlled herself and wouldn't allow her emotions to go too far. "Everywhere I look, I'm reminded of him," she said softly. "This house is too big for me. Bob used one of the bedrooms for an office. He also had a shop . . . that's where he was when he had the heart attack . . ." Ginny started to weep softly, then again regained control of her emotions.

"That's OK," Angela said. "We don't mind if you cry. It's normal — and healthy."

"Thanks. You don't know how much I appreciate that. This neighborhood has been so good to us. I wish we'd gotten involved. Bob was not very outgoing. He liked to do his projects and read. We rarely had people over . . . just a few friends who liked to play bridge. I don't deserve all of this generosity."

"We want to help. Really."

"But I can't pay you back."

"That's not the point. You need us right now and we *want* to help. We don't expect anything in return."

Ginny sighed. "I wish I'd made more friends. I haven't worked since my son was born. Most of my friends were on Bob's side." She shook her head.

Angela suddenly shifted to the edge of her seat. "I've got an idea! I'm going up to the mountains next weekend. My parents have a cabin there and I go up once in a while just to relax. It's really a beautiful place, right on a lake. Why don't you come with me. It might be good for you to get out of the house for a couple of days."

Ginny's face brightened. "You really mean that?"

"Yes. Please come. We'll have a good time."

"What about the house . . ."

"My roommate will be glad to keep an eye on it. Robin's told me she wants to do something to help. I'll ask her to pick up the paper and the mail for you; even water your plants if you'd like."

"Let me think about it. Maybe that is a good idea, just to get away."

Ginny's face then clouded over and Angela noticed that something else was obviously of great concern. "What's wrong?" she asked.

Ginny shook her head, trying to deny the problem. "Oh, I don't want to burden you."

"It's not a burden."

"My husband didn't have a very current will. There's a number of things I just don't understand, and I don't want to bother my son

. . . he has so much on his mind. But I don't understand some of my husband's documents. Bob handled all of our financial affairs. He believed that was his job and he never told me anything about them."

"Do you have a lawyer?" Carol asked.

"No, I don't. Do you think I should get one?"

"You'd better find out what the law says about his estate. It may not be that complicated, but you need to know where you stand. Since I work in a legal office, I'd be glad to see if one of the lawyers can help you. All three of them can handle this kind of situation."

"I can afford to pay. That's not a problem," she said.

"I understand. You just don't know who to call. Let me take care of it tomorrow. I'll call you to schedule an appointment."

"I do appreciate that. I'm sorry you have to go to all this trouble . . ."

"Ginny, it's no trouble."

A few minutes later, after they'd finished their tea and banana bread, Angela and Carol excused themselves. Ginny escorted them to the door and then, in a spontaneous display of affection, gave each of the women a warm embrace. Again she fought the tears as she tried to express her thanks. "You don't know what your visits mean to me. You've all been so kind."

Suddenly she remembered, "Oh, I need to return your dishes. Let me get them."

Carol suggested that they could also return dishes to the other neighbors. "Let us take care of that for you."

"Well thank you. Tell them I really appreciated the food. I wasn't up to fixing meals and this helped. I'll be sending them thank-you notes."

As Angela and Carol left, each carrying a small cardboard box of serving dishes, Carol said they might as well drop off Amy's casserole dish right away.

Sue was visiting with Amy when the doorbell rang. Amy invited the neighbors in and her guests returned dishes to Amy and Sue at the same time. "We just spent some time with Ginny," Angela explained.

"How is she?" Sue asked.

"She's holding up well, but she is very lonely."

"Angela invited Ginny to go to the mountains with her next weekend," Carol explained.

"She needs to get away and rest, without any responsibilities," Angela added. "Also, Carol offered to help get her some legal assistance."

"She's really worried. She's not prepared to live alone. Her husband took care of all their financial matters, so she feels lost."

"I'd think that would cause anyone to worry," Sue agreed. "I'd certainly be afraid if Clark died."

"That's true. But unfortunately we can't always avoid bad circumstances," Amy said. "Sometimes we get caught in them, and we can worry or fret, or learn to deal with them. Angela and Carol, you've done some very practical things to help her."

"I wish she could see that she has a lot of good life ahead of her," Angela said.

"She will. First she'll have to get through the grieving process; then she can begin to learn how to deal with her worries. You're helping her, and maybe all of us can contribute."

"What could I do?" Sue asked. "I've never lost anyone close to me. I feel so inadequate in this situation."

"That's normal. Let's think about it, though." Amy invited the women to sit down for a minute. "Worry is something we all battle. I know I did for years . . ."

"I really appreciated what you told me the other night," Carol interrupted. "I read that booklet and it was very helpful."

"Carol's talking about our discussion on the day Bob died. Sue, you and I have talked about this before, about how our relationship with God is foundational for handling anxiety and other problems in our lives." Amy continued: "Carol, you demonstrated a concrete action to help Ginny with this specific anxiety. When Ginny said she was worried about her legal problems, you offered to arrange for her to meet with a lawyer. What you did was eliminate that cause for worry."

"I hadn't thought about that. But you're right, that is a good way to deal with worry. The other day I visited my obstetrician . . . by the way, I felt the baby move for the first time! What a thrill that was."

For a couple of minutes, the ladies were diverted in their conversation by talk about the health of Carol and the baby in her womb. While they talked, Ted arrived and greeted the women. "We were just talking about Ginny and how we could help her," Amy said.

"Mind if I join in? I've been concerned about her, too."

After Ted was seated, Carol resumed her original thought.

"We were talking about eliminating the cause of worry whenever possible. I was saying that the other day I had a number of concerns to discuss with my doctor. I wrote down a list of questions: Am I gaining weight too fast? Is it all right to eat pizza? Should I take aspirin when I have a headache or is that bad for the baby? When my doctor asked me if I had any questions, I was ready. She answered each of them, so I didn't have to worry anymore."

"You don't have to give up pizza, do you?" asked Angela.

"Well, she did suggest that I go easy on it. It contains a lot of salt and too much salt makes my body retain water. She told me that it would be better to use a pain reliever other than aspirin. But she wasn't too worried about my weight. So really, I eliminated any reason to worry in those areas. But I've started a new list!" Everyone laughed.

Sue noted that sometimes it's not possible to eliminate the cause of worry. "I mean with Ginny. She still has lost her husband. She must have concerns about income, companionship, and so on."

"That's true," Amy agreed. "We can't always eliminate the cause of worry. After my father died, I found myself thinking a lot about him and Mom. I couldn't change the fact that he had died. But those thoughts were so painful, I found it was better to substitute other thoughts for them. Instead of constantly thinking about how Dad was gone, it was far better to listen to good music, play the piano, or pray for Mom. Angela, you're helping Ginny a lot by taking her with you to the cabin. It won't change her situation, but it will give her something else to think about. She'll see some nice scenery, be with a friend . . ."

"Are you planning to do anything up there?" Ted asked Angela.

"What do you mean?"

"Like taking a hike, going for a drive, going out for dinner. It might not be too good for her just to sit around the whole time."

"Oh, right! I enjoy all of those activities and yes, we'll do some fun things."

Amy noted that Carol might soon be learning a technique for displacing thoughts. "Are you planning to take a childbirth preparation class?"

"Manny and I are signed up. The class starts in three weeks."

"One of the things you'll learn is how to take your mind off your pain. Among the techniques they teach are breathing exercises. As you concentrate on your breathing, you don't think as much about the pain of your contractions."

"About Ginny, I wonder if I could help her do some planning for the future," Ted offered. "That's a good way to displace fearful thoughts."

"I don't think she knows what she wants to do. Her life was wrapped up in Bob. So maybe you could help her there."

"Would it help to let her talk?" Sue asked. "I'm home every day. I could take the kids over and visit her two or three times a week. Maybe that would cheer her up. And if she wants to talk, well, people say I've got good ears."

"That makes a lot of sense," Ted smiled. "I have found that a good way to help a person displace her present grief is to let her reminisce, talk, and remember the good times."

Carol said that while these ideas were good and practical, sometimes we still can't get the thoughts of worry out of our minds. "I mean, Ginny can't change the fact that her husband is gone. She's going to be reminded of it daily for a long time. I guess I wonder what I'd do in that situation . . ."

"Maybe then you just treat the symptoms; keep it from getting out of control," Angela suggested.

"What do you mean by that?" Ted asked.

"I guess I'm thinking of keeping things in perspective. She had thirty-five good years with Bob. I hope she will see that she has twenty or more good years ahead of her, and that there are lots of things she could do. It doesn't change her circumstances, but it might help her cope with her grief. I heard her say once that someday she hoped to do volunteer work in a hospital. Wouldn't that give her life some meaning, to help others?"

"That's a very good point," Amy agreed. "Ginny would be good at that. She's quiet, but you know she cares."

Sue added that often it's through difficulties that we grow in character. "I don't know quite how to say this, but I think the difficult times, when I look back on them, have been the times when I've matured the most. I think of when Clark left baseball and was struggling to earn enough to pay the rent. We learned a lot during that time. Does that make sense?"

"You're so right," Amy nodded. "Another thing that helps me gain perspective is to think of the worst consequence of my problem, and why that wouldn't be so bad. Sometimes it's little things that cause me the most worry. Last year we were getting ready to go on a week-long vacation. My hair dryer was on its last legs and I spent a couple of hours worrying about what I would do if it died on the trip. Finally I thought, 'This is silly to waste time worrying about such a minor thing. What is the worst thing that could happen?' I decided the worst thing that could happen was that my hair dryer would break during the trip. What would happen then? I'd have to let my hair dry naturally and it would be quite curly. Now that wasn't so bad. Ted had seen me that way before and he'd still love me. And if I determined I really needed to get another dryer, I could do so, though it might cost a few dollars more than if I bought one here in town on sale. My point is that when I thought about the worst that could happen in that situation and what I would do if it did happen, there was no longer any reason to waste my energy fretting about it."

Ted gave another illustration from work that explained how he relieved some of the pressures of his job. "Sometimes I feel like an overloaded pickup truck. You've seen them occasionally on the highway, loaded down with furniture, riding low on the springs with the tires looking almost flat? The truck can't go too far under that load, and neither can our bodies constantly handle too much pressure. For me, the pressure builds when I have stacks of work on my desk and I'm not really sure what's in them. I know I'm behind and I can't possibly get to everything that day. But I feel a whole lot better when I take a few minutes to go through the stack and find out what I have to do and plan how I'm going to attack it. The work still needs to be done, but I've at least gained some perspective."

"I've got another idea," Angela said. "I find that one way to treat my anxiety is to have a good workout. I'll go swimming or take a brisk walk or jump rope for a few minutes. It also helps to eat good foods and I take extra vitamins."

"Clark often relieves my anxiety with a joke," Sue said. "It's crazy, but I'll be uptight and he'll get me laughing and pretty soon I'm relaxed again." Sue checked her watch and noted she had to go. "By the way, Clark wants to have a Super Bowl party for all the men. So, Ted, you're officially invited. So is Manny. I'm inviting all the women, too. For those who don't want to watch, we'll have some fun of our own!"

That night, Ted wrote in his journal about the discussion concerning worry. He thought of the ideas they had exchanged and jotted some words on his paper. "How to deal with worry," he thought aloud. "Eliminate the causes. Displace the thoughts. Treat the symptoms. Hmmm. That's E, D, T. What's another word for Eliminate. Delete? Aha! *DDT.* That's a good way to kill the things that bug us!" Ted looked at his new acrostic:

DEAL WITH WORRY

- **D** ELETE the causes
- **D** ISPLACE the thoughts
- **T** REAT the symptoms

He thought about those three principles and realized he could apply them right away. Lately, he'd allowed some of the pressures of work to build, causing him to worry. He was anxious about an upcoming sales training conference he was organizing. He was also worried about his teenage son who was facing new problems with peer pressure. *What can I do about those?* he wondered.

He wrote down his ideas. Under *Delete the Causes,* he believed he had planned every detail of the training conference. He could delete that cause of worry by reviewing once more all of the details, confirming the schedule of the speakers, and reviewing with his assistant the responsibilities she would have in handling the logistics with a local hotel.

Under *Displace the Thoughts,* he realized that he was expending too much energy thinking about the things that could go wrong with his son. He decided that when an anxious thought came up about his son's friends, he'd use that as a prompting to review the many good influences in his son's life. Most of those friends were actually pretty good kids. They were all active together in sports. And he and Amy had worked hard to teach their son to develop his convictions and stand on his own. As far as *Treating the Symptoms,* he decided he needed to spend some extra time with his son so they could talk "man to man" and gain perspective on the new pressures. He also decided to resume his jogging program that had been sidetracked because of his hectic schedule. At least three mornings a week, he'd take half an hour for hard exercise.

Just writing down these thoughts made him feel more at ease. He leaned back and reflected on how for many years anxiety had prevented his wife from achieving her potential. It had robbed her of energy and limited her ability to think and focus. In recent years, she had come so much closer to fulfilling her potential because she had learned to deal constructively with worry. And now that Amy was no longer constantly burdened with worry, she really was enjoying life more.

That's what was so good about this project. Ted and Amy were benefiting as much as their neighbors. They were reminded of old truths and also learning new principles that helped them achieve their potential and enjoy life. Now, as Ted closed his notebook, he anticipated the Super Bowl when he could spend some time with the men on Fir Court.

Learning to like what you have to do.

11

ICE CREAM ACTIVITIES

"**S**uper Bowl or Super Bore?" Ken muttered as the first half of the Super Bowl ended.

"Clark, your TV practically puts you in the game," Ted added. "Thanks for inviting us over."

"Too bad the game isn't more interesting," Clark apologized. "It looks like another blowout."

Clark then invited the men into the kitchen where Sue had laid out toppings for banana splits. "Maybe this'll spark up the second half. Gentlemen, sundaes! Let's see who can make the biggest. We've got plenty of ice cream."

"Save some for us!" came Sue's voice from the living room. Several women were chatting after having watched the first few minutes of the game. The men began to build incredible splits. Manny and Ken's were most impressive. Manny heaped up a half dozen scoops of ice cream and smothered them with caramel, chocolate, fudge, nuts and cherries. Ken's was only slightly more modest, with only one topping — several spoonfuls of fudge — over a mound of ice cream, all blanketed with whipped cream.

As they made their way back to Clark's family room and the big screen TV, the men eagerly attacked their creations. At first no one talked as the Super Bowl half-time extravaganza continued. But, with the score already lopsided, few were interested in the show. Ted was one of the first to finish. He noticed Manny relishing every bite and said, "I don't think I've ever seen anyone enjoy his ice cream more than you do."

The others provided some good-natured kidding. "I'd sure want to be on your team for any eating contest!" Clark laughed. And Sam added, "Where do you find room for all of that good stuff?"

Manny enjoyed the attention. "I've always appreciated good food. And now with my wife pregnant, you know, I've got to sympathize with her. I can't let her eat alone."

"Of course not! You wouldn't think of letting her suffer by eating pizza and pickles and hot fudge sundaes without help," said Ted with a grin. "Hey Manny, do you ever get tired of eating ice cream?"

"Never. I wouldn't mind eating it every day."

"If ice cream had all the basic nutrients you needed, do you think you could live on it?"

"You bet. What a way to go!"

"It's unfortunate that everything we do isn't as much fun as eating ice cream."

"Uh-oh. Time to talk about our potential again," Clark noted.

"I was just thinking that there are some things that simply aren't much fun to do. You might call them 'liver activities.' They kind of sit on the plate and quiver."

"Yuck!" Ken exclaimed, who was digging up the last scoops of liquid ice cream and fudge.

"And because we don't like to do them, often we don't do them well. Certainly that limits our potential. But what if there were some way of taking those liver chores and turning them into ice cream activities?"

"I like that idea! Do you have any suggestions?" Sam asked.

"A couple. It's something that's intrigued me and I thought it might be fun to brainstorm."

Sam added, "I'll tell you one thing, my job sure isn't a whole lot of fun. I wouldn't mind finding some ways to make it more enjoyable. Take those athletes on TV, for instance." The two teams were beginning to return to the field. "Now they have it easy. They get to play a game, and make a lot of money doing it. And look at the respect they get. It must be nice being a pro athlete."

Clark couldn't help but laugh at Sam's analysis. "Boy, are you naive. I've been a pro athlete, and I know a few pros. Believe me, most of the time it ain't glamorous."

"That's right, you played ball, didn't you?" Manny asked.

"A year and a half of minor league baseball. And I was in the most minor of the minors, a Class A rookie league."

"Didn't you enjoy it?" It was Ken, who had secretly always wanted to be a pro athlete but didn't have the athletic skills.

"At times. The games were fun, especially when you played well. But the rest was pretty grueling. We had to be at the park three or four hours before each game. There was hitting practice, fielding practice, drills in the fundamentals, and conditioning. After the games you'd try to find a place to eat, and sometimes that was hard. Besides, most of us didn't have much money. Half the time you were on the road, and those eight-hour bus rides get old in a hurry. Fans only see the games; they don't see the hours of sweat and drudgery that go into preparing for those games."

"Why did you do it if it wasn't that much fun?" Sam asked.

"All of us did it for the same reason. We wanted to play in the major leagues. We knew if we didn't practice and learn from our coaches and continue to improve, we'd never make it to the big leagues. We endured the long bus rides and the long hours because we knew almost every big league ball player had gone through the same process in order to reach the majors."

"So the dream of the major leagues motivated you to keep going when you didn't feel like it," Manny concluded.

"Yes. That's why we were there."

"Clark, one of your statements gives me an idea," Ted noted. "You said you didn't enjoy the drills, but the games were fun. What if you could take some of those things that aren't much fun — those liver activities if you will — and make a game out of it? For example, Clark, I'll bet you did that sometimes in baseball practice. Didn't you try to simulate game conditions?"

Clark thought for a moment. "That's true. In batting practice, the coach often called out a game situation and we had to hit accordingly. 'One out, runner on third,' he'd say, and I'd try to hit a sacrifice fly. Or 'runner on second, none out.' My job was to hit to the right side of the infield to advance the runner."

"I did similar things when I played sports in high school. In basketball, we had to shoot fifty free throws at the end of every practice. I kept track of my percentage and wrote it down. I'd always try to beat my current average. Another way I made a game of it was to compete with a teammate. We'd try to see who could make the most free throws."

Ted then announced a "fun" new exercise program. "Here's how it works. Start at one point. Take ten steps forward as fast as you can. Then take three rapid steps sideways one way, six rapid steps sideways the other way. Then return to the starting point at a walk. Repeat this for one hour. How about it?"

"Sounds boring," said Ken.

"Well, suppose I call this program *tennis?*"

Ken laughed. "I do play tennis, and you're right, it's pretty much the way you described. It's just that I've never stopped to think about it because I'm having so much fun playing the game."

"Wouldn't the same idea work in our jobs if we tried to make a game out of some boring chores?"

"Do you make a game out of your job?" Sam asked.

"Sometimes. Let me give you an example. One thing I don't like to do is make phone calls. There's always a stack of calls to make, and often the calls I do make generate more calls, and it's an unending cycle. So one thing I've done is keep a tally of the number of calls I make and receive each day. Every time I dial a number, I get a point. Even if I dial the wrong number or information, I give myself a point . . ."

"Hey, you can't do that!" Ken protested.

"Why not? After all, Ken, it's *my* game and I can play it any way I want!" Everyone laughed. "My personal record is fifty-five calls in one day."

"Memos!" Sam said. "That's what I hate. Sometimes I think our company is about to choke with all the memos we send each other."

"What's the most you've ever gotten in one day?"

"I have no idea."

"Why not keep track?"

"You could have records for every day of the week!" Clark suggested. "And for a one-week total, and one month."

Sam couldn't help but laugh at Clark's enthusiasm. "I see your point. I actually do a similar thing with my production staff. We'll sometimes see if we can beat our production record for the previous week just to make things interesting."

"So you can do the same thing with memos," said Ted. "Making a game of it could make your job a little more bearable."

Clark was watching the TV screen. "Speaking of games, did you see that play!" The conversation stopped for a few minutes as the men watched the replay of a 51-yard pass. But when the dominant team extended their lead even more, all interest in the game waned.

"I was just thinking of another way to enjoy something you have to do," Clark said. "I had a good friend when I was playing minor league ball. Andy and I were from very different backgrounds, but for some reason we clicked. While he played more than I did, it was obvious his career wasn't going to last much longer than mine. We spent a lot of time together, encouraged each other, ate meals together, sat together on the bus, warmed up our arms by playing catch with each other, even did our wind sprints and calisthenics together. When he got discouraged, I'd tell him to keep trying. When I was down, he told me not to give up."

"I know what you mean," said Manny. "Most of the time when I drive truck, I'm alone. When it gets boring, I get on the CB and there are three or four buddies I often talk to. We keep each other in stitches at 3 o'clock in the morning. They've helped me stay awake more than once."

"I like that," Ted said. "You just gave me an idea. There's a proposal I have to write this next week, and it's in an area where I just don't have a lot of interest. I've been procrastinating, but this week I've got to get it done. I think it would go much easier if I did it with someone. I have a friend down the hall who's pretty good at this kind of project. I think I'll ask him to meet with me for an hour and see if I can't get some help on it."

"What if you can't get someone to work with you," Sam groaned. "A lot of my work has to be done by me. The boss wouldn't like me wasting other people's time on it. Besides, they'd slow me down, anyway."

"I think that's true at times," Clark said. "There are some things we just have to do ourselves. But sometimes we can do it with others, and when we can, that makes it more fun. I have a friend who wasn't making good grades in college until he met this girl he really liked. She was always studying in the library, and since he wanted to be with her, he would go to the library with her every evening. And while he was there, he decided he might as well study. Guess what? His grades went up!"

Ken chuckled at the example. "Hey, if I found a really sharp single woman, I just might go back to college." The group laughed and kidded Ken about his priorities.

"I think Sam raised a good point," Ted said. "There are some things we simply can't do with friends, that can't be made into a game. You just have to do it."

"Right. And it isn't any fun," said Sam.

"Not always. Hey look, my team's actually moving the ball!" With less than five minutes to play, the losing team was putting together an admirable drive toward the goal line. But a fumble inside the fifteen yard line ended the drive as the defensive team pounced on the ball. A collective groan rose from the men.

"For a moment they looked good," Ted said. "I think the reason why is applicable to our discussion."

"If they'd played like that earlier, they might have had a chance," Manny said.

"Notice both sides seemed to be putting out more during the last few minutes. The goal of winning the Super Bowl motivated them to give the extra effort. Their goal became even clearer as the end of the game approached. When we have a goal firmly in our minds, that can motivate us to reach our potential, too. Clark, I noticed a picture of a bikini-clad woman on your refrigerator."

"Sue put that there. We're going to Hawaii next month for a sales convention. She wants to lose five pounds so she'll look good in her bathing suit."

"So that picture reminds her of her goal and helps her stay out of the fridge."

"I've wondered if I should put a picture of a hippo in a bikini *inside* the refrigerator. Then when she opened it, she'd see what she might become if she spent too much time in there."

While Clark laughed at his own joke, Ted noted, "Either way the goal is clearly in mind. Sometimes we forget *why* we're doing something, and then it's very hard to enjoy it. I think that's what I hear Sam saying; his job has become tedious."

"Boring."

"OK, boring. But I don't think it has to be. When a task obviously contributes to some valuable objective, we usually find it quite interesting. But it becomes boring when we don't see any reason why we should do it. Clark, you told us you endured the times of drudgery and worked hard during your drills in the minor leagues because you knew it was the only way to make progress toward your ultimate objective — the major leagues. That's why it's important to remember why. Now, let's see if there's a similar motivation for Sam's job. Why do you work there, Sam?"

"I've asked myself that question many times."

"Why did you go to work there originally . . . what was it, about twelve years ago?"

"Thirteen. I needed a job."

"Why did you take that job?"

"It had decent pay, good benefits, and steady work. I was an equipment operator, but there were opportunities for advancement. However, now I've gone as far as I can with this outfit."

"But your original goals have materialized?"

"Yeah, I guess that's true."

"A couple of years ago we had a downturn in the economy. Were you out of work during that time?"

"No, it didn't affect our business."

"Clark, how about you? How did you do during that recession?"

"Awful. Schools cut their budgets and one of the areas they cut was new athletic equipment."

"So Sam, while others were suffering, your job kept right on going. It didn't even affect your income. So your original objectives for getting the job were achieved. And they still hold — decent pay, good benefits, and steady work."

"I guess you're right. I do have a lot to be thankful for."

"That's my point. We often get discouraged with something we have to do because we forget why we're doing it."

"I see your point. But I think there can also come a time when the reasons why you did something don't apply as much any more. Perhaps you have new objectives. However, I certainly could have been happier with my job in past years if I'd thought about why I was there. Now, I'm finding more of my thoughts focused on starting a cabinet shop."

"You ought to quit now if you're not happy," Ken said to his father.

"How would we pay the bills?"

"I could work with you. With both of us using our contacts, I think we could do quite well."

Sam shook his head. "I don't know. I'd like to believe you're right."

"There's the gun!" Clark interrupted. On the screen, the victorious team was lifting their coach to their shoulders. Fans were pouring onto the field. Television cameras invaded the winning locker room where exuberant players were hugging each other and whooping their delight.

"This was fun!" Manny said. "However, I think our discussion was far better than the game."

Ken commented, "Typical Super Bowl; it never quite matches the media build-up."

"Well, you're all invited back next year," Clark said. "Maybe it will be better."

That evening Ted reviewed the discussion and made a note on his Monday "To Do" list to schedule an appointment with his friend to work on the proposal. As he thought of the ideas the men had discussed, he tried some combinations and finally wrote:

LEARN TO LIKE WHAT YOU HAVE TO DO

- **G** O back to "why"
- **E** NLIST a friend
- **M** AKE a game of it

Now there's a gem, he thought. A gem is valuable. And when you enjoy what you're doing, life becomes more valuable. Corny? Perhaps. But he wouldn't forget it. He'd have to share that with his friends so they'd remember, too.

Ted thought about the times when he was most productive, when he was closest to achieving his potential. Those were the times when he was motivated. He could work long hours without loss of energy. And then there were times when he wasn't as motivated and thus not as productive. At those times he found he didn't enjoy life as much either. *Wow!* he thought. *These are three powerful ways to stay internally motivated.*

Then he thought of all he had learned in the past few months. Maybe it was time to pull these ideas together and see what he had. He knew he would spend all of his life learning new ways to achieve his potential and enjoy life. But periodically he wanted to review his progress, so that the principles remained fresh and applicable.

He grabbed a yellow note pad, turned back to the beginning of his notebook and started to read. As he read, he began to construct a chart . . .

*The neighborhood finds out how
far they have progressed in helping one another achieve their
potential and enjoy life.*

12

PUTTING IT
ALL TOGETHER

It had been almost a year since that momentous July barbecue.
Six of the seven households had actively participated in Ted's "project."
Actually, they no longer saw it as "Ted's thing." Just as good neighbors
lend a hand in an emergency or borrow each other's tools or an egg
or a cup of sugar, so this neighborhood willingly exchanged ideas
that would help one another achieve their potential and enjoy life.
Of course, they all realized they were a long way from perfect, but
they were certainly closer now than if they had never taken up the
challenge.

Now one of the families was leaving. Sam, Julie and Ken were
moving to another community several miles away. The three of them
had talked a great deal in recent months, ever since Sam had broken
the ice and revealed his dream to operate his own cabinet shop. They
had found an ideal place for the shop. It was an old home with
plenty of room for them to live, and a large addition that could hold
all of Sam's equipment and two work benches. Julie would continue
her job, but Sam was reducing his hours. He would work part-time
as a production consultant, which allowed him to preserve much of

his pension and other benefits. The rest of his time would be spent doing what he enjoyed most — building quality cabinets and furniture. Ken was proud that his father had taken this bold step and had already lined up several jobs for them as soon as they moved into their new home.

The party was in the back yard behind Ted and Amy's house. Manny and Carol were showing off their baby, almost three months old now. Manny had wanted a boy and that's what he had, an eight-pound son named Manuel. "Manny II," Clark called him. The women took turns holding the little child — including Ginny, who was an enthusiastic participant in the party.

After the meal, Manny suggested a group photo. "Before the Turners break up the world's best neighborhood, let's get a picture of everyone." The group assembled on the patio and shifted according to Manny's instructions. He placed his camera on a tripod and set it for a ten-second delay, then ran to join the picture. Despite good-natured protests, he did this three more times to be sure he got a shot with everyone smiling.

Ted then asked everyone to be seated. "One year ago, I suggested that we exchange ideas that would help us all come closer to fulfilling our potential and enjoying life more. I promised that I would then make a report. Well, with our dear friends leaving, the time has come. Here are the basic techniques we came up with to help us achieve our potential and enjoy life. They are grouped into four broad categories — *directional, operational, relational, and motivational.*

"As I review these with you, I'll be asking some of you to explain how you've applied these principles. Then when that's done, we want to make a special presentation. The first major grouping consists of *directional skills.* They're first because in order to achieve our potential, we need to know where we're going. We need to identify the finish line. We discussed with the Appletons how to maximize the use of our strengths."

Ted had prepared a large flash card for each concept and he held up the first one:

MAKE THE MOST OF **YOU**

- **Y** OURSELF—Discover your strengths
- **O** BJECTIVES—Determine where you're going (your goals)
- **U** SE—Make good use of your strengths and your opportunities to reach your objectives

"We agreed that in order to reach our potential it is essential that we know our strengths, clarify our objectives, and then, in light of our opportunities, use our strengths to help us achieve our objectives. Clark and Sue, would you like to tell us how this concept helped you?"

"I believe this was probably the most important thing I learned," Clark began. "I didn't realize I was drifting so much. Without any clearly defined direction, I was living according to whatever felt best at the moment. Fortunately, I like my job and I love my family, so I did accomplish quite a bit. But when I think about reaching my potential, there's a lot more I can do. I thought of a comparison; do you mind if I share it?"

"Please do."

"I could compare my life to a gallon of gasoline. If I pour it out on the ground and light it, there will be a big, spectacular flame for a moment or two. Then it will die out and that's it. However, if I pour that one gallon of gasoline into an economy car, I can drive thirty or forty miles, maybe more. Putting the gas in the car accomplishes a lot more. I've realized that I can waste a lot of time and energy only doing what feels good at the moment. Or I can channel my efforts to reach some desirable objectives."

"And I will say, my husband is definitely more directed now," Sue said. "Earlier this year, we left the kids with friends for a weekend and went to a nice hotel where we spent a lot of time talking about our strengths and discussing our goals and objectives. We've decided to do that at least once a year. One area we've planned is what to teach our children this year. That's really helped because now Clark and I are working on the same plan, so we're much more consistent as parents."

Ted was obviously pleased as he listened to the Appletons' report. He moved on to the next principle.

"This next concept came out of a discussion among the women. From them, we learned how we can fulfill more of our potential."

GROW TOWARD YOUR POTENTIAL

- **T** RY—Be open to grow and learn new skills
- **B** UY—Make a good decision on what to apply
- **A** PPLY—Plan to implement your decisions

"My roommate can tell you how that's helped her!" Angela said.

Robin, while still shy, was now very comfortable among these friends. She reported about her night classes at the community college. "I've been taking some computer courses that relate to my job. My company is paying for that. But I also took a course in business administration just because I wanted to. And now, I'm thinking of going on and working toward a college degree, either in computers, or business administration, or who knows — maybe both! I'm listing my objectives in order to make a decision chart."

Angela added a little more information about her roommate. "Robin is much more disciplined now that she has some goals. And she views her job not just as a way to get a paycheck, but also as a vehicle that is helping her blossom as a person."

Sam told how his wife had suggested they use a decision chart before they decided to move and start the new business. "That was so very helpful, because it allowed us to get all the important facts down in front of us. We had basically three alternatives, and several objectives."

"We did the chart as a family," Julie added. "I think that's making the move easier, because we all had input, and we all see how the decision was made."

"I agree that the decision chart and then the follow-up planning to help apply the decision was a major concept," Ted said. "Alice, thank you for sharing that with us. Now we move into the second major area, the *operational* principles and system that help us accomplish our objectives and implement our decisions. We realized very early that in order to reach our goals, we needed to manage our time. Sam, you were a great teacher in this area. You gave us four basic principles that are represented by the acrostic *NAPS*."

MANAGE YOUR TIME

- **N** OTE commitments right away
- **A** RRANGE your standard day or week
- **P** UT everything in its place
- **S** TART and finish top priorities first

Ted gave the first endorsement of these concepts: "I realized that I had two systems for handling my appointments — one for work, the other for family. I don't know why I didn't think of this sooner, but I suddenly realized I'd be more efficient if I combined them. Why not have one schedule book that I keep with me all the time?" Ted showed the group a small, leather schedule notebook. "This fits neatly in my suitcoat pocket. On the first page I've written my goals, on the second my standard work day. Then I have my calendar — one week on a page with room to record my commitments. Finally, in the back, I have a pad where I keep my 'To Do' list."

Sue also had a report. "Sam, you'd be proud of Clark's desk. This was really a tough area for him. But he's forced himself to keep his desk organized. Every evening he sorts the mail. He has files for various catalogs, new product information, and so on. He uses the slots of that organizer you built for him so he stays on top of the clutter."

"I'm still not up to Sam's level," Clark laughed. "I have my lapses. But now rather than letting the mess build up over several weeks, I rarely go more than three or four days before I attack the pile. And, rather than spending an hour or more digging through the mess — and sometimes I never would find what I needed — it feels so good to be able to find things quickly."

Alice told how she had also refined her system. "Sam and Julie repeated their course for me. I'm amazed how much I accomplish now just by having a good set-up. My stationery business is run from a desk next to the kitchen. I have a large calendar on which I schedule my parties and the phone calls I need to make. My kids had me put up a section for each of them on a bulletin board above the desk. If there is something I need for them to do relating to the business, I pin it on the board and they check it each day."

Ted thanked everyone for their contributions thus far, then continued. "Next we talked about a persistent problem for many of us who have children — interruptions. We discussed how we can even take advantage of those situations."

ROLL WITH THE BENEFITS

- **R** ECOGNIZE the positive side of interruptions (the benefits)
- **E** MPLOY your natural tendencies
- **D** OUBLE up on your time

"Carol, we talked about that in the context of your job. How is it going now with the baby?"

"Manuel is a fussy baby at times. He wants to be fed every two hours, and he's not sleeping through the night yet. Some nights, I'm up three or four times. I think if I hadn't learned this concept, I'd be very frustrated. But you know what I've done? When he wakes me up at night, I now look forward to that time when it's very quiet and I can just enjoy my son. It won't be long before he's feeding himself and sleeping through the night."

"We probably all remember our Christmas celebration," Ted said. "That night, we talked about how hard it is to persevere in all of these areas. We agreed that to achieve our potential we need to follow through."

FOLLOW-THROUGH

- **P**ERSISTENCE—Keep at the important things until you're done
- **A**CCOUNTABILITY—"Report" to someone
- **D**ISCIPLINE—Implement despite feelings

"That's helped me," said Ken. "I tend to be kinda hang-loose. Starting this business with Dad is showing me that I must be more disciplined. I can't just do what I want, when I want."

Clark agreed. "My desk is proof that I can change. I realized that my messiness was simply a bad habit, and if I wanted to change and was disciplined and persistent, I could change. It took a few months, but now I'm in the habit of keeping my desk organized."

"I'm learning to say no!" said Julie. "I'd lo-o-ove to do it, but I can't! That seemed like a silly exercise, but it was exactly the discipline I needed. Occasionally I still take on more than I should, but it's definitely more manageable."

Ted now moved into the third area, *relational* principles. He displayed the acrostic *CHAT* that was developed partly during a neighborhood brainstorming session, and partly through an evening with the Turners. "In order for us to achieve our potential, we have to work well with people. This is a reminder of the primary elements we've said are necessary in order to have quality, mutually satisfying relationships."

ENJOY "QUALITY" RELATIONSHIPS

- **C** ARE—Let people know they are important
- **H** EAR—Listen until you understand
- **A** FFIRM—Let people know they are doing well
- **T** ELL—Communicate clearly and sensitively

"In addition, we discussed how for important communications it helps to plan ahead so we can *tell* effectively."

TELL—COMMUNICATE CLEARLY AND SENSITIVELY

- **W** HAT do you want to say?
- **W** HY do you want to say it?
- **W** HO are you talking to?
- **H** OW should you best present it?
- **W** HEN should you say it?

"May I say something about that?" It was Ken, who couldn't wait to give a report. "A year ago my dad and I weren't communicating well at all. In fact, whenever we did talk, it often ended with us shouting at each other. I want to say that Dad's changed. Well, maybe I've changed some, too. For the last few months, we've had a lot of good talks, and we rarely get upset at each other any more."

"The house is definitely more peaceful," Julie agreed. "Ken, tell them about your negotiations on the business."

"Before we decided to start this business together, Dad and I examined it from every possible angle. We looked at our individual strengths and weaknesses, and we talked about realistic goals for the first year, second year — all the way to five years. We discovered that our differences may well be an advantage. For example, I'm going to do more work soliciting business and scheduling shows, while Dad will be responsible for ordering supplies and quality control. However, one thing we decided was that we'd definitely work better if we had two benches. I'll never measure up to my dad's standard of neatness. So I'll have my bench, he'll have his, and he's agreed not to get on my case, no matter how my bench looks."

Sam shook his head and smiled as his son talked. "I guess that is a real change for me. I realized I was trying to make my son be just like me. But Ken's not like me. He's unique. He's got different strengths. And while he allows me to contribute to his life, I need to let him be who he is."

Ted felt a tug of emotion in his throat. This was a family that seemed ready to crumble a year ago. Now it was functioning in harmony. He continued, "We also dealt with the issue of worry. This moves us into the *motivational* area and two final concepts. Several of us agreed that we struggle with anxiety. Amy, why don't you address that."

"Ted's asking me because I tend to be the worrier in our family. But I've learned that worry doesn't accomplish much of anything. In fact, it robs me of energy to do what I want and need to do. It keeps me from achieving my full potential. Sue, Carol, Angela, Ted and I talked about three ways to deal with worry . . ."

DEAL WITH WORRY

- **D**ELETE the causes
- **D**ISPLACE the thoughts
- **T**REAT the symptoms

"Could I comment on that?" It was Ginny, and everyone was eager to hear what she had to say. "This is the first time I've heard all this, and I realize I've missed a lot by not being involved more with the neighborhood. But Angela, on that weekend she took me with her to the mountains, told me about your discussion on how to deal with worry. And I certainly saw you putting it into practice with me. I want to tell you that it works — it really does! I don't know what I'd have done without you."

Ginny found herself fighting tears and her friends were moved by her openness. "Since Bob died, I've thought about selling my house — I simply don't need all that space — and moving into a condo. But I've decided not to do that right now. I want to stay here and get to know all of you better — and learn more about these concepts."

Angela was sitting next to Ginny and she gave her neighbor-friend a warm hug. "I'm so glad you're staying," Angela said.

"And now, for the Super Bowl finale," Clark said. "This is where the men really performed. We learned the fine art of building banana splits." The group laughed at Clark's animated announcement. "Actually, those banana splits led to some good ideas on how to enjoy everything in life — even though some part may be unpleasant."

"That's right," Ted said. "I don't know if it allows us to like everything. But we discovered that we can learn to like many of the unpleasant things we have to do in life."

LEARN TO LIKE WHAT YOU HAVE TO DO

- **G** O back to "why"
- **E** NLIST a friend
- **M** AKE a game of it

"Do you know how many memos I've had to read?" Sam asked. "I figured it up and in the last five months I've had to read more than 2,000 memos. I have started keeping a tally sheet and adding it to my weekly report." Sam chuckled as he told the following story. "The company president visited my office last week and said, 'Sam, are you trying to tell us something?' I said, 'What do you mean?' 'This thing about the memos. Have we really had that many? That's an average of about twenty a day!' 'That's right,' I said. He was quiet for a moment and then he said to me, 'I wonder if that means we're not as efficient as we should be.' I didn't say anything to that. I just listened."

"Congratulations!" Clark said. "You took something you didn't like and made a game of it, and in the process, you may actually change things."

"Well, I'm not holding my breath. The issue is not that they will change, but that I learned to live with the situation."

"That completes the four groupings," Ted continued. "However, there is one *foundational* concept that I believe underlies all that we've talked about this past year. And this is it."

LOOK TO GOD FOR PEACE AND WISDOM

Ted looked at Amy. She walked over to the Turners and said,

"Sam and Julie, we're sure going to miss you." She was surprised at her deep feelings. Yes, she had to admit she loved the Turners almost as if they were part of her own family. "And so you won't forget us, we've put together a little memento from all of your neighbors on Fir Court." She handed a package to Julie.

Julie unwrapped the present and found a chart of the principles Ted had just presented, penned on parchment and matted and mounted inside an oak frame. "This is beautiful," Julie whispered. Her eyes moistened. "Thanks so much. This will hang in a very prominent spot in our new home . . ."

"So we won't forget what we've learned," added Sam. "You know, Ted, I'm glad you made that foundational principle very clear on the chart. It really is the most important part . . ."

Sam's voice trembled, and he had to stop for a moment to gain his composure. "Gee, this sure isn't like me . . . Ted, I want to thank you and Amy for helping me find the hope and peace of mind we can have in Christ."

He stopped again, this time to try to think of exactly the right words. "I can look over this chart and see so many things that are helping my life right now. I've got a far better relationship with my son and wife. I have direction for my life. I've learned how to communicate more effectively, and how to handle worry constructively. But of all of those things — good as they are — establishing my relationship with God was most important. That's what has made the rest of these principles work in the best possible way." He gave a little chuckle and concluded, "I might add that God still has a lot of work to do in me!"

This was a very tender moment and everyone was moved. Everyone had noticed the change in Sam's life. Julie broke the silence by saying, "Ted and Amy, thank you. Really, you have been so loving and helpful. I mean, it wouldn't have happened without you."

"Here, here!" said Clark as he started to clap. The rest of the group joined in and gave a warm ovation to this special couple. As the applause ended, Clark added, "Hey, Sam and Julie, we're going to miss you. But you can spread the news of what you've learned here. Maybe you can do a similar project in your new neighborhood."

"That's right," Angela added. "This is too good to keep to ourselves. If this has meant so much to us, then let's help others who might want to know how they can achieve their potential."

Alice quickly added, ". . . and enjoy life!"

* * *

Do you want to achieve your potential and enjoy life?

You can. What happened on Fir Court can happen in your neighborhood. It can happen in your home. It can happen in your life.

Maybe you're wondering, "Where do I begin? There were so many principles covered in these pages. I can't do them all at once."

That's why we've added a few more pages to help you use these principles. First, there's a Reader Workshop to help you start to apply these principles to your own life and situation.

Next, you'll find the chart Ted and Amy presented to the Turners so you can see all of the concepts at once. You might want to photocopy the chart and put it in a place where you can review it regularly.

Finally, there is a copy of the contents of the booklet that Ted gave to Carol and Sam. We hope it will be helpful to you.

It was our desire that you would enjoy reading this story. Even more, we wanted you to gain some helpful ideas that you can apply in your own life.

We want you to achieve your potential and enjoy life!

APPENDIX A
READER WORKSHOP

Do you really want to achieve your potential and enjoy life more? Then you need to start now.

Most people implement only a small fraction of the lessons they read or hear about. Why? Often they forget about them. They let the press of other activities squeeze them out of their schedules. Most of the time they never even start on them.

We don't want that to happen to you this time. And, apparently, neither do you.

Take a few minutes right now to read the next few pages and do what they say. You will be on your way toward achieving more of your potential.

FIRST, "BUY INTO" SOMETHING.

As you read this book you became exposed to many possible new ways for you to think and act. Take out a sheet of paper or a 3 x 5 card and write down the several principles or techniques that seem like they would be the most beneficial for you to apply soon. All the main points of the book are summarized on the chart in appendix B. Looking at that chart may stimulate your thinking.

Once you have several possibilities written down, pick *one* as your first project. "Only *one?*" you may ask. Well, it is better to do one than to think about many! Besides, it will take some time and energy to get one going. Don't risk overloading yourself and quitting. When the first one becomes a habit for you, go back to your list and implement another one.

So, which one lesson do you need to apply the most? Put the number "1" alongside it on your list.

SECOND, PLAN TO APPLY IT.

In chapter 5 you saw a very simple way to plan to apply: *what/ how/when.*

Let's take that outline and use it to help you plan to apply. On your sheet of paper, or on a second 3 x 5 card, write the answers to the following questions:

1. *WHAT* exactly do you hope to do differently?

Let's take an example to clarify. Suppose that someone named George has a number-one priority to manage his time better. *NAPS* is the acrostic for that. But, to be more specific, George *really* wants to learn to be more organized in his schedule and around the house. So his goals may be expressed:

WHAT — *Establish the following habits for my life:*
1. **N**ote *commitments right away.*
2. **A**rrange *my standard day.*
3. **P**ut *everything in its place.*

Now it's your turn. Write down what exactly you hope to accomplish with your number-one priority.

2. *HOW* should you try to accomplish it?

In our example, George has three parts to his "what." So he selected the "best way" to start on each part:

HOW — *1. Buy a pocket appointment calendar I like.*
Keep it out in front of me, on my desk at the office and on my dresser at home, until I form the habit of noting all my commitments in it.
2. Try out doing different schedules of activities — at home and at the office — and see how productive and satisfied I am with them. Select the best one as the "standard day" I can shoot for.
3. Have a family day to clean up the garage. Buy some metal shelves for added storage. Ask Dave how he reorganized his garage.

Notice how George determined "hows" for each part of his three "whats." In each case, he wrote down a few simple steps that he hoped would get the job done. He could always add steps later if he had not yet achieved his goal.

Also notice how he anticipated when he would need more sources. On his third point, for example, he hoped to involve other family members, saw the need to spend some money on new shelves and planned to get some advice from his neighbor who had just gone through a garage reorganization. Bringing appropriate resources to your project is a crucial point of "how."

Now, write down "how" you plan to implement the "whats" in

your number-one priority. Leave a little space between each point.

3. *WHEN* should you do these things?

George wrote the word "when" alongside "how" and added some deadlines in parentheses after each point:

> *HOW/WHEN — 1. Buy a pocket . . . all my commitments in it. (Buy calendar tomorrow.)*
> *2. Try out doing different . . . "standard day" I can shoot for. (Try this Monday through Friday for the next two weeks.)*
> *3. Have a family day . . . his garage. (Possible "Clean Up" day: July 26. Ask family and confirm.)*

Don't skip this point. Many plans become idle dreams because they never get into the schedule. Take a moment to add "when" to your plans.

Now let's review for a moment. You have selected one top priority for you to apply and you have written a plan to accomplish it. Congratulations! You are way beyond a typical New Year's resolution.

Chances are you will do what you have planned . . . *but* you may not. Why? Because there are some very predictable barriers you may face. That leads to our third main point in this workshop:

THIRD, OVERCOME THE BARRIERS.

Barrier 1: "Losing" your plan before you get started.

Just because you wrote it down doesn't mean it has made it into your schedule yet. Let us suggest two ways to overcome this barrier.

A. Put the "when" of your plan into your commitment calendar. If you already have a reminder system, use it. Your plan's deadlines are probably more important to you than many other things you might do with your time. If you will need a few evenings to begin doing your plan, schedule those evenings right now.

B. Keep your plan in sight. Whether or not you did "A" above, do this. The best way to harness the activities of a day toward your plan is to read over the plan every morning. Put the plan where you will see it in the morning. Think of what you can do today to make progress toward your new habits. Pray and ask for God's help.

Barrier 2: "I don't like what I have to do."

Perhaps the reason you need to implement your number-one priority now is because you have been procrastinating doing something about it earlier. Often we procrastinate because we don't like what we must do.

How can you overcome such a huge barrier? Do you remember from chapter 11 three ways to learn to like what you have to do? They are:

A. GO back to "why"

B. ENLIST a friend

C. MAKE a game of it

If you run into this barrier, reread chapter 11 and think of some specific ways you can learn to like the unlikable part of your plan.

George, for example, could remember why he wanted to change: *(1) So I won't forget to show up for important appointments; and (2) So things are not in the way around the house.*

Barrier 3: "I'm afraid I might fail."

That's true; you might. But if you don't try, you will "fail" for sure. You will not see the personal growth you desire.

How can you overcome fears and worries? Chapter 10 gives you three ways to deal with worry:

A. DELETE the causes

B. DISPLACE the thought

C. TREAT the symptoms

Reread and apply that chapter when your fears slow you down.

One other important thing: "Look to God for peace." Your relationship with God is foundational to experiencing peace in spite of your fears and concerns. Reread chapter 9 and appendix C if you have some questions about your relationship with God.

Barrier 4: "I never can follow through on what I start."

Join the club. We all struggle with follow-through.

If you run into this barrier on your project, go back to chapter 7 and see how you can apply one or more of the following three key principles:

A. PERSISTENCE — Keep at the important things until you're done

B. ACCOUNTABILITY — "Report" to someone

C. DISCIPLINE — Implement despite feelings

Barrier 5: "Just when I start, I get interrupted."

Yes, people don't always "happen by" according to our plan. That's life. So what can you do about it when it seems to keep you from making progress on your plan?

Remember how to "Roll with the Benefits" from chapter 6:

A. RECOGNIZE the positive side of interruptions (the benefits)

B. EMPLOY your natural tendencies

C. DOUBLE up on your time

The next time you see "RED" because of an interruption, try these ideas.

Barrier 6: "I never seem to get around to it."

Is there a person alive who hasn't said this? So what can you do?

Start now! "Now?" you say. Yes, *now.* Determine something — anything — you can do right now on your plan. Can you make a phone call to enlist some help? Can you put a copy of your plan where you'll see it each morning? Can you pray for it? Can you take a few minutes to think about how to "clean the garage"?

The chances of your implementing your plan diminish in proportion to how long you wait to start.

Some years ago, my then four-year-old daughter Debbie had managed to get my two-year-old Michelle caught in her little "walker" chair. Michelle couldn't escape and apparently started crying. Debbie rushed out to the kitchen and said to me, "Dad, could you get Michelle out of the chair?"

I was just finishing eating and said yes but did not move right away. Debbie asked again, "Dad, could you get Michelle out of the chair?" I said yes but again didn't quite sense the urgency. Immediately Debbie said a third time, "Dad, could you get Michelle out of the chair?" Again I said yes, but before I even had a chance to say more, Debbie exhorted, *"Well then, do it!"*

You have read the book. You have your plan for your number-one priority. You know how to deal with the barriers you may face. You stand to fulfill your potential and enjoy life more if you follow through. So, for your sake, my final encouragement is: "Well then, do it!"

KEY WAYS TO HELP YOU ACHIEVE YOUR POTENTIAL AND ENJOY LIFE

DIRECTIONAL	OPERATIONAL

MAKE THE MOST OF YOU

YOURSELF—Discover your strengths

OBJECTIVES—Determine where you are going

USE—Make good use of your strengths and your opportunities to reach your objectives

GROW TOWARD YOUR POTENTIAL

TRY—Be open to grow and learn new skills

BUY—Make a good decision on what to apply

APPLY—Plan to implement your decisions

(What, How, When)

MANAGE YOUR TIME

NOTE commitments right away

ARRANGE your standard day or week

PUT everything in its place

START and finish top priorities first

ROLL WITH THE BENEFITS

RECOGNIZE the positive side of interruptions (the benefits)

EMPLOY your natural tendencies

DOUBLE up on your time

FOLLOW THROUGH

PERSISTENCE—Keep at the important things until you are done

ACCOUNTABILITY—"Report" to someone

DISCIPLINE—Implement despite feelings

CHART DECISIONS

		Alternatives		
		A	B	C
Objectives	1	+	-	+
	2	0	0	-
	3	+	+	0

RELATIONAL

ENJOY "QUALITY" RELATIONSHIPS

CARE—Let people know they are important

HEAR—Listen until you understand

AFFIRM—Let people know they are doing well

TELL—Communicate clearly and sensitively

TELL—COMMUNICATE CLEARLY AND SENSITIVELY

WHAT do you want to say?

WHY do you want to say it?

WHOM are you talking to?

HOW should you best present it?

WHEN should you say it?

MOTIVATIONAL

DEAL WITH WORRY

DELETE the causes

DISPLACE the thoughts

TREAT the symptoms

LEARN TO LIKE WHAT YOU HAVE TO DO

GO back to why

ENLIST a friend

MAKE a game of it

FOUNDATIONAL

LOOK TO GOD FOR PEACE AND WISDOM

APPENDIX C

Here is the text of the booklet Ted gave to Sam and Carol. It is from an actual booklet that has helped many thousands of men and women achieve their potential in the all-important spiritual dimension of life.

HAVE YOU HEARD
OF THE
FOUR SPIRITUAL LAWS?

Just as there are physical laws that govern the physical universe, so are there spiritual laws which govern your relationship with God.

LAW ONE

GOD **LOVES** YOU, AND OFFERS A WONDERFUL **PLAN** FOR YOUR LIFE.

GOD'S LOVE

"For God so loved the world, that He gave His only begotten Son, that whoever believes in Him should not perish, but have eternal life." (John 3:16).

GOD'S PLAN

(Christ speaking) "I came that they might have life, and might have it abundantly" (that it might be full and meaningful) (John 10:10).

> Why is it that most people are not experiencing the abundant life? Because. . .

LAW TWO

MAN IS **SINFUL** AND **SEPARATED** FROM GOD, THUS, HE CANNOT KNOW AND EXPERIENCE GOD'S LOVE AND PLAN FOR HIS LIFE.

MAN IS SINFUL

"For all have sinned and fall short of the glory of God" (Romans 3:23).

Man was created to have fellowship with God; but, because of his own stubborn self-will, he chose to go his own independent way and fellowship with God was broken. This self-will, characterized by an attitude of active rebellion or passive indifference, is an evidence of what the Bible calls sin.

MAN IS SEPARATED

"For the wages of sin is death" (spiritual separation from God) (Romans 6:23).

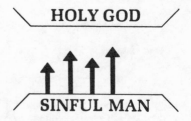

This diagram illustrates that God is holy and man is sinful. A great gulf separates the two. The arrows illustrate that man is continually trying to reach God and the abundant life through his own effort, such as a good life, philosophy or religion.

> The Third Law explains the only
> way to bridge this gulf. . .

LAW THREE

JESUS CHRIST IS GOD'S ONLY PROVISION FOR MAN'S SIN. THROUGH HIM YOU CAN KNOW AND EXPERIENCE GOD'S LOVE AND PLAN FOR YOUR LIFE.

HE DIED IN OUR PLACE

"But God demonstrates His own love toward us, in that while we were yet sinners, Christ died for us" (Romans 5:8).

HE ROSE FROM THE DEAD

"Christ died for our sins. . .he was buried. . .He was raised on the third day according to the Scriptures. . .He appeared to Peter, then to the twelve. After that He appeared to more than five hundred. . ." (I Corinthians 15:3-6).

HE IS THE ONLY WAY TO GOD

"Jesus said to him, 'I am the way, and the truth and the life; no one comes to the Father, but through Me'" (John 14:6).

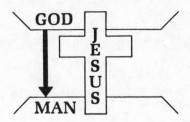

This diagram illustrates that God has bridged the gulf which separates us from Him by sending His Son, Jesus Christ, to die on the cross in our place to pay the penalty for our sins.

It is not enough to know these three laws nor even to give intellectual assent to them. . .

LAW FOUR

WE MUST INDIVIDUALLY **RECEIVE** JESUS CHRIST AS SAVIOR AND LORD; THEN WE CAN KNOW AND EXPERIENCE GOD'S LOVE AND PLAN FOR OUR LIVES.

WE MUST RECEIVE CHRIST

"But as many as received Him, to them He gave the right to become children of God, even to those who believe in His name" (John 1:12).

WE RECEIVE CHRIST THROUGH FAITH

"For by grace you have been saved through faith; and that not of your selves, it is a gift of God; not as a result of works, that no one should boast" (Ephesians 2:8,9).

When We Receive Christ, We Experience a New Birth

(Read John 3:1-8.)

WE RECEIVE CHRIST BY PERSONAL INVITATION

(Christ is speaking) "Behold, I stand at the door and knock; if anyone hears My voice and opens the door, I will come in to him" (Revelation 3:20).

Receiving Christ involves turning to God from self (repentance) and trusting Christ to come into our lives to forgive our sins and to make us the kind of people He wants us to be. Just to agree intellectually that Jesus Christ is the Son of God and that He died on the cross for our sins is not enough. Nor is it enough to have an emotional experience. We receive Jesus Christ by faith, as an act of the will.

These two circles represent two kinds of lives:

SELF-DIRECTED LIFE

S — Self is on the throne

† — Christ is outside the life

● — Interests are directed by self, often resulting in discord and frustration

CHRIST-DIRECTED LIFE

† — Christ is in the life and on the throne

S — Self is yielding to Christ

● — Interests are directed by Christ, resulting in harmony with God's plan

Which circle best represents your life?
Which circle would you like to have represent your life?
The following explains how you can receive Christ:

YOU CAN RECEIVE CHRIST RIGHT NOW BY FAITH THROUGH PRAYER

(Prayer is talking with God)

God knows your heart and is not so concerned with your words as He is with the attitude of your heart. The following is a suggested prayer:

"Lord Jesus, I need You. Thank You for dying on the cross for my sins. I open the door of my life and receive You as my Savior and Lord. Thank You for forgiving my sins and giving me eternal life. Take control of the throne of my life. Make me the kind of person You want me to be."

Does this prayer express the desire of your heart?

If it does, pray this prayer right now, and Christ will come into your life, as He promised.

HOW TO KNOW THAT CHRIST IS IN YOUR LIFE

Did you receive Christ into your life? According to His promise in Revelation 3:20, where is Christ right now in relation to you? Christ said that He would come into your life. Would He mislead you? On what authority do you know that God has answered your prayer? (The trustworthiness of God Himself and His Word).

THE BIBLE PROMISES ETERNAL LIFE TO ALL WHO RECEIVE CHRIST

"And the witness is this, that God has given us eternal life, and this life is in His Son. He who has the Son has the life; he who does not have the Son of God does not have the life. These things I have written to you who believe in the name of the Son of God, in order that you may know that you have eternal life" (I John 5:11-13).

Thank God often that Christ is in your life and that He will never leave you (Hebrews 13:5). You can know on the basis of His promise that Christ lives in you and that you have eternal life, from the very moment you invite Him in. He will not deceive you.

MEET WITH OTHER CHRISTIANS

The Christian life was not meant to be lived alone. God's Word admonishes us not to forsake "the assembling of ourselves together . . ." (Hebrews 10:25). Several logs burn brightly together; but put one aside on the cold hearth and the fire goes out. So it is with your relationship to other Christians. If you do not belong to a church, do not wait to be invited. Take the initiative; call the pastor of a nearby church where Christ is honored and His Word is preached. Start this week, and make plans to attend regularly.

SPECIAL MATERIALS ARE AVAILABLE FOR CHRISTIAN GROWTH.

If you have established a relationship with God through Christ as you were reading the above, please write me and tell me about it. I would be delighted to send you some materials that will help you in your ongoing walk with God.

Steve Douglass
c/o Here's Life Publishers
P. O. Box 1576
San Bernardino, CA 92402

4-505-1375

Kamala 4-755-0624

Sabrina 4-362-9860

4-758-7928

Paula 4-525-8456

W
strengths

Goals
within 5 years I
want to have
annual sales of
5 million Dollars
company top sales
person next 3 yrs
3rd To ~~have~~ get 2
designation each year

Call past clients
within
within 5 yrs
run a successful
Real estate Business
Help Barry increase
anual sales top
sales. million dollar
Business
Increase production

Target mailing 500
apartments, homes
for listing
300 letters weekly.
Call friends, cards
family aquaintances

Pattie Pate

4-314-0642 (c)

4-899-4108